The characters and events

in this book are fictitious.

Any similarity to real persons,

living or dead is coincidental

and not intended by the author.

" TO ALL THOSE WHO PICK UP THIS BOOK, THANK YOU FOR GIVING MY WORDS A CHANCE"

TABLE OF CONTENTS

1

Rain (short for Lorraine) and I were at a bar in New York City having the time of our lives. We graduated high school in Delaware a few years ago and saved our money and moved to the big city for some excitement and hopefully to meet a nice guy. We got an apartment together in Nooklyn. The bar was loaded with people and this was our first time, out an about, since we moved here. There were a lot of guys at the bar and we were sitting at a table very close by. We were on our second round of drinks and I told her that we should be careful and not drink too much. We weren't driving or anything, but we didn't want to be so drunk that we didn't know what was going on around us. The place was really loud and there was a lot of talking, laughing and yelling. People were playing pool and throwing darts and other games that were available.

All of a sudden, a fight broke out between two guys at the bar, and they were getting pretty rowdy, violent and aggressive. They were throwing punches and they were close to our table. I told Rain, that we should get up and out of the way and as soon as I got up from the table, I caught a roundhouse in the head and I felt myself bending backwards and I felt his knuckles hit me. I woke up on the floor with a lot of people around me. I could taste my own blood and everything was all blurry. Rain was yelling to me, "RENEE, RENEE, WAKE UP." I heard her but everything was all fuzzy and I passed out again. I came to again and had a blood pressure cuff on me and there were paramedics around me. One of them was talking to Rain.

Their voices were all muffled and inaudible and I didn't know what they were talking about. A guy got in my face and kept saying, "I'm sorry, I am so sorry hon. That punch was not meant for you. I am so sorry." But his voice was all muffled. The paramedic asked him to get out of the way and he had a flashlight in my eyes and I was blinking. I heard more muffled sounds and I saw his mouth moving, but I couldn't make out what he was saying to me.

They put me in an ambulance and put oxygen on my face and he was still talking to me. He and his associate were watching me and kept taking my blood pressure and asking me questions, but I couldn't hear them. It seemed like I was deaf now and the voices weren't muffled anymore. I couldn't hear anything. Then the driver put the siren on and I jumped a half a mile and all of a sudden, I could hear and started crying uncontrollably. One guy was close to my face and said, "It's ok hon, you are ok, What is your name hon?" I heard him and said, "Renee, Renee Madden." He smiled at me and said, "Ahh your back. You are gonna be alright. Just relax and we will get you all fixed up."

They continued to the hospital and rushed me into the emergency room and everything started sounding muffled again. I couldn't talk to them and say that, I couldn't hear them. What was happening to me? The paramedic looked into my eyes again with the flashlight and said something to a nurse leaning over me.

They were rolling me around and I felt dizzy and then sick to my stomach and I think I threw up. They were turning me on my side and I thought I heard someone say that I had a concussion. They kept me in that position for a while and they kept talking to me to keep me awake.

The paramedic that talked to me in the ambulance the whole time, stayed with me and his co-workers left. He was holding my hand and I looked at his name badge on his shirt. It said, "Vincent." The doctor finally came in and they rolled me out of the room and took me to x-ray. When I got back, Vincent was still there and Rain was in the room waiting for me. She had a scared look on her face. She leaned over me and said, "You ok Nay Nay?" I could hear her, but I couldn't talk. I opened my mouth and nothing came out. She started crying. Vincent told her I would be ok and sometimes that happens after getting hit in the head. He took my hand again and was holding on tight. "You will be ok hon." He looked at Rain and said, "What the hell happened in there anyway?" She told him that there was a bar fight and I caught a punch. He said he knew that, and was wondering if she knew anything else about the fight and she told him she had no idea.

Rain asked him if he was off-duty and he said he was and that this was his last call of the day. He kept looking at me and checking on me the whole time he was there. He was touching my forehead and smoothing my hair.

After a couple hours went by, I started feeling better and Vincent was still there holding my hand and he told Rain to go home and get some rest and he would be here. He stayed with me the whole night. I am not sure why he was still there, because I didn't know him. He seemed very concerned and kept talking to me about his family and his friends and how many calls he had during the day and about his calls and the stupid things that people did and he would laugh intermittently. He was trying to keep me awake, I guess. He had a very soothing voice and I was interested in everything he had to say. I didn't talk to him, but I was listening intently to everything.

Do paramedics normally do this? Ya know, like, stay with their patients all night? I don't think so, from what I knew about them. I mean, I never read up about them or anything, but I don't think this was normal.

Finally, he stopped talking to me and the nurses were in and out, taking my blood pressure and checking on me. He said, "You can sleep now hon. I am going to go home now and you will be in good hands. Try to stay out of trouble ok?" And he chuckled at me.

I must have dozed off and when I woke up, it was noon the next day. Guess who was sitting there at my bedside? Yup, It was Vincent. He was back and he was holding my hand and watching TV. He looked at me and said, "Good Afternoon Hon. You made it through the night and you will be fine." What did he mean by that? Was I at risk of dying and that is why he was still there? I tried to talk to him and said with a shaky voice, "Was I going to die?"

He bent over me and said, "It was a close call for a while, but you are gonna be ok. I promise. You took a good shot in the head. There is no internal bleeding. Thank God for that." He smiled at me and then said, "They are going to take you for another x-ray to make sure and then you will have to stay a couple days to make sure everything is ok, but I will be here for you." I looked puzzled at him and said, "Why? Why will you be here for me. I don't know you, do I?" He laughed and said, "No, you don't know me yet, but I promise, you will. *You caught my eye* hon." I smiled at him.

He was about 6'1" from what I could tell, laying in this bed. He had brown hair, to just below his ears and brown eyes, that sparkled as he talked, and he was cute as could be. I said, "You don't have to work today?" He said, "I have to go in at 5, but I will be back when I get off."

The nurse got me up to use the bathroom and I caught a glimpse of myself in the mirror. One half of my face was bright purple and swollen and my right eye was swollen shut and the right side of my mouth was cut and swollen and puffy. I started crying and the nurse took me back to the bed and helped me get in. He looked at me and said, "You will be ok soon. You just have to rest." I was still sniffing and sobbing. "I am so ugly. OMG." He said, "No you are not and don't say that. You are a very pretty girl or I wouldn't be here. It will heal fast." He handed me a tissue to blow my nose and he wiped my face gently with another one.

My face felt like it was on fire and the nurse gave me an ice pack to put on it. Vincent held it there for about 20 minutes and told me that it would help with the swelling and healing. He said, "The nurses will give you the ice pack every hour for 20 minutes at a time, and I want you to use it because it will help the swelling go down faster." I shook my head. "Why are you here Vincent?" He said, "You can call me Vinnie and I am here because I told you, *you caught my eye*." I just smiled at him.

He left at 4:00 to get ready for his shift at 5 and pecked me on the good side of my face on my cheek. "I am glad you are ok. You scared me for a little bit there." I thanked him for sitting with me and checking on me. He said, "I get off at 11:00 and I will be back. Don't go anywhere ok?" I told him I had no intentions of moving and he laughed.

Rain came to visit and spent a few hours with me. She brought me some flowers and a box of cookies. While she was there, I had 3 deliveries of flowers. One was from Vinnie, one from the bar where this happened and one from a man name Gary. I assumed it was Gary that threw the punch, that caught my head, instead of his opponent, but I wasn't sure. The nurse came in and out and they had to take me for another x-ray to make sure I had no internal bleeding. Vinnie said they would be doing that. Rain was still there when I got back and the nurse said the doctor would be in as soon as the x-ray was read and he would let me know the results.

The nurse brought me another ice pack and told me she would be back in 20 minutes. Rain looked at me and said, "I feel so bad for you. You really got walloped and I thought the guy that hit you was gonna have a heart attack and the guy that was supposed to get it, felt bad too. You ended the fight and I thought they ended you. I was so fucking scared that they killed you." I told her that I heard muffled sounds and couldn't see and that I tasted blood in my mouth and then I couldn't hear anything until they turned on the siren in the ambulance and that it scared me.

She stayed with me for a little while longer and left. I fell asleep and when I woke up the ice pack was gone and Vinnie was there. It was 11:30 p.m. and the nurse brought me another ice pack and some pain killers. Vinnie told me that I looked a whole lot better. I thanked him for the flowers and he gave me a peck on my good cheek. He asked me how I felt and I told him I was much better than earlier. My eye was open and the swelling had gone down a lot.

The doctor came while I was sleeping, so I never got the results of the x-ray. I asked the nurse when she came in and she said she would find out when the doctor would be back, but she was not allowed to give me that information, even if she had it. I asked Vinnie if he knew who Gary was and he said, "Gary was my assistant last night. He is a good guy." I was shocked. "Really? Wow. I thought it was the guy that hit me. Since when do paramedics send flowers to people they pick up?" He laughed and said, "They do when the girls are cutie pies." I said, "Oh stop."

He asked me if I was from New York and I told him I was from Delaware and just moved here a month ago. He asked me where I lived and I told him me and Rain shared an apartment in Nooklyn on Gates Avenue. He said, "I have heard of Nooklyn. That's a nice place and pretty reasonable for New York." I told him it was small but it worked for us. We had some good conversation and I found out he has been a paramedic for 5 years and he was going to school to become a physician assistant. I was impressed with that.

He was 24 years old and he knew what he was going to do with his life. He asked me what I do and I told him that I was a pharmacy technician and that I didn't really know what I wanted to do with my life. I told him I just turned 21 and Rain and I worked and saved money to move here. He said, "You are young and I think you are on the right track. That is an impressive job for a 21 year old. Are ya interested in becoming a paramedic?" I laughed and said, "Me? A Paramedic? I don't know." He said, "Think about it. It's pretty exciting and interesting. That is if you can stand the site of blood." I told him blood didn't bother me, but I only saw little bits of blood, not a lot.

Vinnie left for the night to get some sleep. I knew he was tired, because he didn't get a lot of sleep the night before. He said he would be back and I believed him. He spent a lot of time with me and he seemed really interested in me. I was kinda interested in him too. He was the first guy I met since moving here, so I wasn't gonna jump into anything right away.

The next morning, I was greeted by Dr. Zhang and he told me that my x-rays were good. There was no internal bleeding and I was good to go home. "We can get you out of here by 1:00 p.m. Does that sound good to you?" I said it was fine and I would call my friend to pick me up. I thanked him and he walked out.

I was getting ready to call Rain, when Vinnie stepped into the room with 2 coffees from Dunkin Donuts. "Hey, Good Morning. I hear you are going home today. You want me to take you? I am free." I smiled at him and said, "Ok, that would be great. Thank you." He leaned over to kiss me on the cheek and said, "Wow, you look so much better today. The swelling has really gone down. Are you still using ice packs?" I told him that the nurses stopped bringing them in during the night, so he went to get one for me. "You really need to keep using them as long as possible and you will be back to normal in no time." I thanked him and he sat there holding it for me. I told him he didn't have to hold it, but he insisted.

The nurse came in with some ibuprofen for me and some breakfast and saw the ice pack. "Oh good, you have one already." And she pointed to it. They were very attentive to me the whole time I was there and I thanked them for that.

I ate some scrambled eggs, bacon and toast and sipped my coffee. "Thanks for the coffee Vinnie. I appreciate it so much. The coffee here (and I whispered) *sucks.* He laughed and said, "I know."

The nurse peeked in again and said they were getting my release papers ready and I could get dressed whenever I was ready, but release time was 1:00 this afternoon and no sooner. I shook my head and said, "Ok, Thanks."

I told Vinnie I couldn't wait to go home and take a shower and get clean. He looked surprised and said, "They didn't let you take a shower?" I told him that the nurses washed me up and they told me they didn't trust me in the shower because I was a little unsteady on my feet. "But I am ok now. I get up and use the bathroom by myself and I am fine." He looked at me and said, "Ok, good. I didn't know you were unsteady." I told him that the punch really did a job on me and he said,

"Yeah, that guy really hauled off on you and you are so little. Well, he was a big guy. You know what I mean." He turned on the TV and the nurse came in to take my dishes and he looked at me and said, "Today is my day off. I could stay with you if you want, or do you want to be alone?" I told him that I really didn't want to be alone and that Rain was going to work at 3:00, so he could stay with me if he wanted to. He smiled and was so happy with my answer.

I texted Rain and told her that Vinnie was bringing me home because he was here and she texted back and said, "Ok, but I am here if you need me or change your mind." I sent her a thumbs up and thanked her.

I got up after an hour or so, and went in the bathroom to get dressed and brushed my teeth and my hair using the stuff that the hospital gave me. They gave me everything, including deodorant. So I packed everything up in the bag they gave me and brought it out. I still had on the slipper socks they gave me and I left them on till it was time to go. I had blood on my sweater from my lip, but I would get that out with a little hydrogen peroxide.

Vinnie looked at me and said, "You are so cute." I blushed and said, "Stop it." He said, "No, I mean it. You really *caught my eye* Renee. I like you a lot." I said, "You don't even know me." He smiled and tilted his head and said, "I will though, I will, I promise and you will know me, you will." I smiled at him and I believed every word he just said to me.

We had another hour before I was allowed to leave. The nurse and doctor came in to talk to me and I signed the release papers. They wrote me a note for work and didn't want me to return until next Monday. They gave me Ibuprofen to take for pain and they wanted me to rest. Not in bed, but no jumping around, no exercise. I sat on the bed and Vinnie was in the chair by my side and we waited for 1:00 p.m. A nurse came in with a wheelchair and I said, I didn't need one and she said it was protocol and that I had to leave that way. I got in and she wheeled me to the front door and Vinnie went to get his car.

He drove around to the front and he got out and opened the door and I got in. He asked for my address and he put it in his GPS. He had a yellow Ford Mustang. It was an older model, but it was cool looking and I loved it. I just had a Mazda that was about 5 years old, but I loved that too.

2

He drove to my apartment and parked in the lot and came up with me. Rain opened the door for me and we came in. Vinnie said, "Do you girls want me to order some lunch? Rain, did you eat yet?" Rain told him she didn't eat yet and she would love some lunch and I shook my head yes. We all decided on Five Guys and he ordered and had it delivered. We all sat at our little round glass kitchen table and had lunch together. Rain looked at Vinnie and said, "It was so nice of you to take care of Renee, but do Paramedics usually do that?" He smiled at her and said, "No we don't usually do that, but you have a really cute roommate." He laughed and said, "She *caught my eye.*" Rain laughed at him and said, "Yeah, I thought something like that was going on."

Rain thanked him for lunch and said she had to start getting ready for work. Vinnie asked her where she worked and she told him, "I am a second shift, receptionist for the Quality Inn near Sunset Park. I work till 11:00. He said,

"Wow, I am impressed with both of you. You both have good jobs. Most girls your age work at a bar or as a waitress or something." She laughed and said, "Thanks, I gotta go get ready." She took off into her bedroom and Vinnie got up and got rid of the wrappers and bag. "Do you need me to take your garbage out? It's pretty full now." I said, "Yeah, if you don't mind. That would be great." He said, "I saw a dumpster in the parking lot. Is that where I put it, or do you have another place?" I told him to put it in the dumpster. He took the garbage out and I put a new bag in while he was gone. When he came back, Rain was leaving for her job and I told him I was gonna go take a shower and he could put the TV on if he wanted, or I had a playstation he could play with. His eyes lit up and said, "Playstation of course." I turned it on for him and he settled in playing a game and I went to take a shower.

I looked at myself in the mirror and started tearing up. I looked horrible and ugly and I wanted to cover up my whole face. I ran some cold water on my face and then took a hot shower and it felt so friggin good. I got out and got in a pair of sweats and came out.

Vinnie asked if I had an ice pack and I went to get it out of the freezer. I started to tear up again and I was feeling bad for myself. He looked up from the game and said, "Aww. You are ok. Don't cry. It will be gone in a week." He dropped the controllers and pulled me in for a hug. It felt good to be hugged because I haven't been hugged in a long time. And I think the last time I was hugged, was by my mom. He held me tight and told me everything was gonna be ok. I needed this bad and he really did make me feel better. I think he was loving it too.

He had his arm around me for a long time and we switched over to TV and watched it for a while. I dozed off for a little while and when I woke up, he was still holding me and watching TV.

Vinnie told me about his mom (Rosa) and his Dad (Jay) and his brother (Jimmie), while we were sitting on the couch. They all lived in Upstate New York and Jimmie was married with a little boy named Kyle and his wife's name was Maria. He told me that he and his brother were like best friends, but they didn't see each other a lot and he missed him.

Rain came home around 11:30 and he left and said he would see me tomorrow.

The next morning around 10 a.m., Vinnie showed up with 3 coffees and breakfast sandwiches and donuts for all of us. I had just gotten out of bed a half hour before that and I looked in the mirror and I actually looked a little better than last night. He looked at me and said, "Oh yeah, look at this, you look so much better." And he pointed to my eye. I pointed to my lip and told him that it was still killing me, especially when I was eating. He said, "Yeah, that was pretty bad when we picked you up the other night. They should have given you a tiny stitch, but it will heal and you will look totally fine." Vinnie came everyday before his shift and every night after his shift was over, for a whole week.

I was supposed to go back to work on Monday, but my face was black and blue and yellow and I really didn't want to go in like that. I sent a picture of my face to my boss and told him what happened to me and he suggested I take more time and he would approve it. I had sent the return to work form to him when I got out of the hospital but didn't say anything about why I was out. He was a nice boss and probably the best one I ever had. He was concerned about me and actually sent me flowers that afternoon and he told me on the phone, that he had no idea what was going on with me. "You take whatever time you need to heal up and your job will still be here when you get back. Don't worry about a thing ok?" I thanked him and told him I would take another week and see what I looked like after that. "If it's not too bad, I can cover it with makeup so I don't scare your customers" and I laughed.

Vinnie said that it was a good idea that I took another week off to heal and he was happy about it. He bought me lunch every day while he was visiting. If Rain was there, he bought for her too. He told me his classes were gonna start up again, in another week and he wasn't sure how many times he would be able to visit me. "Between work and classes, I am gonna be pretty busy and I am gonna miss seeing you. I will do my best though."

The week went by so fast and he was there everyday, late morning and every night after work. I wondered when he ever got to sleep, but he said he slept when he left me at 1:00 a.m. and slept until 9:30, so he got plenty.

When his classes start next week, he said he would be attending them from 10:00 a.m. to 2:00 p.m. He was doing part-time to start because of his job and he wanted to see how it panned out for him. My hours at the pharmacy were 8:00 - 4:00 p.m. with a 1/2 hour for lunch, so I would only get to see him at night after he got out of work.

I went back to work the following week and covered my remaining black and blues with makeup and my boss was happy to see me and told me that if at any time I didn't feel good, to let him know, and he would let me go home. I would never take advantage of that, because he was so nice to me and he paid me for both weeks that I was out.

On my second day of work, I went out to get lunch at 12:00 and Vinnie was at the exit door waiting for me. He had lunch for me and he took me by the arm, pecked at my cheek, and we ate lunch in his car. He didn't have a class today and said he needed to see me. He pulled me close and gave me kiss with an open mouth and got me excited. He said, "I had to see you. I don't like this shit that we both have to work and never see each other."

Of course, it was only one day, but he was upset because he just spent the last 2 1/2 weeks with me almost all day. He said, "I miss the fuck out of you." I told him that I missed him too, but there was no way I could take any time off from work. "My boss was so nice and paid me for both weeks off, so I can't take any time off," He looked at me and said, "Oh no, I would NEVER ask you to do that. I just miss you and I am sad."

I was gonna kiss him on his cheek, but he turned his face toward me and kissed me on my lips. He said, "How do you feel? You are lookin' good girl. Have I told you lately that you are beautiful?" I laughed and said, "You tell me everyday, but when I look in the mirror, I don't see what you see. I am covering up the black and blues and yellows and every other color that my face turned into."

He took my chin in his thumb and forefinger and turned me towards him and said, "You are fucking beautiful and cute as can be, even with black, blue and yellow on your face." He paused for a second and said, "Your lunch is over and I don't want you to be late. I will see you when I get out of work tonight, ok?"

We both got out of the car and he walked me back into the pharmacy and walked with me till I got to the counter. He gave me a kiss and said, "See ya later." I told him to have a good day and he left. My co-worker, Gloria, said, "O..M..G.. girl. He is a fucking cutie pie. Where did you find him? Does he have a brother? Holy Shit." I laughed and said, "You won't believe me if I told you." She said, "Try me." I told her, "When I got punched out at the bar, he was one of the paramedics and he has stayed with me every day since it happened." She opened her mouth in shock. "For real? Jeez. Maybe I should get punched out at a bar." She started laughing and said, "Just kidding, but GOD, he is so cute and I can tell he loves you, just the way he looks at you. Don't let that one go." I told her that he is upset because he doesn't get to see me as much anymore with me working now. I told her that he works from 5-11 and now he is taking classes to be a physician's assistant.

I saw a customer come up to the counter, so I cut the conversation short and went to take care of my customer. Every chance Gloria got to talk to me, she asked me questions about him. I was thinking to myself…why does she want so much information on him? I better not tell her anything else because I really didn't know her too well and didn't know what she was up to.

She was nice, but I didn't know if I trusted her. She asked me questions all afternoon about him and I just kept saying, "I really don't know." Now she was making me uncomfortable and I told her that she was, and she backed off a little. She was creeping me out, because she never talked to me before, until he came into the store.

I told him later that night what happened and he told me not to trust her with anymore information. "Especially like, where you live or I live and shit like that. That is just fucking weird." I agreed with him and told him that all she knows, is how I met you and that you are a paramedic and you are taking classes on-line. I told him I didn't volunteer anymore information and just told her I didn't know. I told him I was nervous around her now and that I hoped that I didn't give her too much information already. He told me not to worry about it.

We spent a couple hours together and he went home to get some sleep. He told me he had a class the next day from 10-2 so he couldn't meet me for lunch but he said he would see me tomorrow night after work. He told me that he had the whole weekend off and had no classes and wanted to know if I wanted to get together. I told him I had to work Saturday morning from 9-1, but then I was available the rest of the day and all day on Sunday. He said, "Oh ok, Wanna grab some dinner with me Saturday night?" I told him that I would love too. He told me that there was a place called Serafina Tribeca, downtown, that was an Italian Restaurant, if I liked Italian. I told him I loved Italian Food and that place would be great. He said, "Hey, what nationality are you?" I told him I was English and Irish. I said, "What nationality are you? I don't even know your last name." He said, "It's Greco and I am Italian. Well, my Dad is Italian and my mom is Irish."

After he left, I got ready for bed and took a quick shower. I got in bed and started having pain in my shoulder and my neck. It was really bad pain and I was trying to rub it out, but that wasn't working, so I got up and took some Advil. I sat up for about 1/2 hour and waited for it to work, but it wasn't. I went back to bed and rolled around all night with this fucking pain and even cried at one point, because it was so bad. I got up at 7:00 to get ready for work and I realized that I just couldn't make it, so I called in and left a message for my boss and apologized and explained to him what was happening. I texted Vinnie and told him that I wasn't going in to work and what happened after he left. He showed up at my door at 8:15 a.m. with coffee and egg sandwiches. He looked concerned when I opened the door. "What's going on hon? Where is the pain, show me." He walked in and he put the coffee and sandwiches on my table. I pointed to my shoulder and neck and he said, "That is the side you fell on, and you probably got injured when you fell. Sometimes, it takes a few days before you feel the full effects of a fall or injury." He took the ice pack out of my freezer and rigged me up with tape, so it stayed in place. We sat and ate breakfast and sipped our coffees and then he got up and said, "If you don't mind, I brought my laptop and I can do my classes here. Ya got internet here?" I told him that I had internet and I was happy he was gonna do his classes here. I said, "I took Ibuprofen last night and it didn't do anything for the pain." He said, "Ah, ya know what that means?" I shook my head no and he said, "It's because it's not muscle pain. It's nerve pain. Do you have a chiropractor?" I said no and he told me he had one, if I wanted to use him. I told him I never went to a chiropractor and I was scared. He explained to me that it sounds scary, but it feels good and he gave me his number and then he grabbed it back and said, "I will make the appointment for you and I will take you, because I don't think you will do it." And he started laughing. I laughed with him because I knew I wouldn't call it, voluntarily. He said, "OK?" I shook my head yes. He took his phone out and called and made me an appointment for this afternoon. I looked at him and said, "Don't you have to go to work at 5?" He ignored me and then called his boss to take the night off. I said, "VINNIE, NO. Don't do this for me." He looked surprised and said, "WHY? I want to. Be quiet. You need to get this taken care of immediately. The longer you wait, the worse it will be. I know what I am talking about." He paused and then said, "I know I am sounding bossy and I don't mean to be, but you really need to have this looked at babe." He was calling me babe? Ok Wow, what does this mean? I just met him a couple weeks ago. I mean, I knew we had a connection, because I felt it when he hugged and kissed me. I think the only reason I trusted him so much, was that he was a paramedic. Everyone has to trust a paramedic, right?

He went out to his car and brought in his laptop, a book, a pad and a pen attached to it. I gave him my internet password and he got on-line. He said, "There, I am all set up for 10 when my class starts. Can I just sit here at the kitchen table or do you need it? I can use the coffee table if its more convenient for you." I told him the kitchen table was fine. He still had an hour before his class and my appointment was at 3:00 p.m. I said, "Thanks for the coffee and breakfast. I appreciate it. I really didn't feel like making anything this morning." He said, "Of course hon. No problem at all."

My phone rang and it was my boss. He asked me what was going on and I told him that I was seeing a chiropractor at 3:00 and I would keep him updated. He told me to take my time and let him know. I thanked him for understanding.

Vinnie and I were sitting at the kitchen table and he looked up at me and asked, "Are you going to sue the bar or the guy that punched you? You really should think about it, because you are having more problems than what we thought in the beginning. Now, loss of work, medical bills, etc. Don't just brush it off." I told him I would think about it and maybe just the guy that punched me but not the bar. "How is it the bar's fault? I don't understand that." He explained that I could because, they sold the liquor to their patron and their patron lost control because of it. "Just do it. It will be worth your while. I know a good lawyer too. I can give him a call for you if you want.

You don't have to file right away, but you can give him all the details and he can keep track of all your medical bills and such." I said, "You really think I should sue both of them?" He shook his head yes, so I told him to go ahead and call him. I said, "But I don't want you to have to take anymore time off from work." He laughed and said, "Ok, then I will take a few days vacation. It's been piling up and I need to use some anyway." He called his boss back and told him that today would be a vacation day and he would be taking the rest of the week as vacation, as well. Then he called the lawyer and made an appointment for tomorrow at 3:30 p.m. I started laughing and he asked what was so funny. I giggled again and said, "You don't waste anytime doing anything do you?" He chucked at me and said, "Why wait? You need to get this stuff taken care of and I am not a procrastinator. I get it done." I reached across the table and touched the top of his hand and said, "Thank you. I AM a procrastinator." And I laughed.

3

He started his classes and I went in the living room and laid on the couch and fell asleep. I slept for 2 hours and then got up and he was still taking notes and listening to the lesson. I gave him a post-it note asking him if he wanted a tuna fish sandwich and chips and he smiled and shook his head yes. I got busy and made the sandwiches and made up two paper plates for us. I held up a coke can from the fridge and he said yes. He gobbled everything down while still take notes and listening to his class and then I cleaned everything up and went back to the couch. I took my iPad and I continued reading a book I got on my Kindle App.

It was almost 2:00 and his classes were nearing the end and my appointment was in an hour. I brushed out my hair and put on a little eyeliner, mascara, covered a few black and blues and put on a tinted lip gloss. I slipped on my sneakers and announced to him that I was ready. He came up to me and hugged me. "You are the cutest thing I have ever seen." I smiled and said, "Oh stop." He kissed my forehead and stepped away and looked at me. "See, just look at yourself. You are cute."

As he was driving me to the chiropractor, he said, "Can I ask you a question? You don't have to answer if you don't want to." I said, "Yeah sure, what is it?" He asked me, "Do you have parents that are alive and if so, do they know what happened to you?" I put my head down and the tears came. "They are alive and I didn't tell them anything." He rubbed my shoulder and said, "Why, Why didn't you tell them?" I said, "Because they were not happy about me moving away to New York City with Rain and they think she is a bad influence on me and they never liked her, even though she practically lived with us, so they kind of disowned me." I paused and dried my tears and blew my nose. "This is the last thing they want to hear. That I went to a bar with Rain and got punched in the face and ended up in the hospital and they would say, 'I told you so'. So no, I didn't even call them." He had a sad face on as he continue to rub my back as he was driving. "I'm sorry love. That's a tough one and I understand why you didn't tell them, but do me a favor and try to call them at least once a month to let them know you are ok. It's important to keep in touch, even if they are mad or you are mad. OK? They ARE your parents after all and they should know you are ok. Even when parents say they are disowning you or they get mad at you, they still worry, because those are just words and you are still their kid." I shook my head yes. It was quiet for about a mile and then he said, "Almost there." He parked the car a minute or two later and we both got out and walked into the office. I was nervous and he knew it. He put his arm around my shoulder and gave me a little tug. "It will be fine. I promise. He is gentle and won't hurt you." He went up to the desk and got a clipboard with a form for me to fill out. We both sat down and I filled out the form and he handed it back to the receptionist. Ten minutes later, she handed us a little clipboard and told us to wait in Room#4 and put the clipboard outside the door in the slot. He said, "Do you want me to come in with you?" I said yes, as I pulled at his shirt and he walked with me down the hall to Room #4.

Dr. Barclay came in a few minutes later and proceeded to ask me a bunch of questions and I answered all of them. I told him about being punched in a bar and Vinnie filled him in about the hospital and that the pain didn't start until last night. Dr. Barclay told me the same thing Vinnie did. "Sometimes these pains take a few days to show up, especially if it's nerve pain." I told him I took ibuprofen and it didn't help and he shook his head.

He made me stand up and he put his finger down my spine starting at my neckline near my hairline and touched every single disc, all the way to my butt. When he got to the middle of my back, I screamed in pain and he said, "Yup, that's the one that is out of alignment. I can fix that for you. You may need to come in a few times, but I can relieve your pain." He put a TENS unit on my neck for about 20 minutes and left the room and when he came back, he adjusted the middle of my back. I heard a loud crack and he lifted me back up to sitting position and then touched my spine again where it was out and said, "Good, Very Good. Can you come back in on Thursday, same time?" I looked at Vinnie and he already said yes. Vinnie asked me how it felt and I told him it still hurt.

Dr. Barclay told me to put an ice pack on it for 20 minutes, each hour and I could use heat after it, if I wanted to. "You will be back to normal in a few days."

We left the office and Vinnie took me out to dinner at a little family restaurant. It was a small place with about 8 tables and a few booths around the back of the wall. It wasn't the restaurant that he picked, but it was an Italian restaurant. He apologized and said, "With all the commotion, I forgot to make a reservation. I'm sorry. We can do that one another night, if you want to." I looked at him and said, "This restaurant is fine Vinnie. We don't always have to follow a schedule. And after all, I am the one who caused all the commotion." I giggled a little.

The dinner was really good and we got Fried Calamari as an appetizer. He got Penne ala Vodka and I had the Ravioli ala Vodka. He said, "You want some dessert?" My eyes were bulging, I was so full and I said, "Oh God, if I put anything else in here, I will explode." And I pointed to my stomach. He laughed and said he felt the same way. "How do you feel?" I told him I was ok, not great, just ok. He said, "Let's get you home for that ice pack. It's important to take the inflammation down. I have a little homework to do anyway."

He put the ice pack on my back as I laid on my side on the couch and he sat at my kitchen table doing homework. Rain left me a note that she would be home around 10 and she was getting out early today and told me to text her if I needed anything. I thought that was nice. I don't understand my parents as far as her being a bad influence on me. She always has my back and I don't do anything I don't want to. I am my own person and I don't let anyone talk me into something that I don't want to do.

Maybe Vinnie was right. I should call them and let them know I am ok. I don't want to sever my ties with them and deep down, I know my mom and dad love me and they want to hear from me. I will call them tomorrow, but I am not going to tell them what happened to me. Vinnie had the ice pack timed and he pulled it out after 20 minutes and put it back in the freezer. "You want heat or are you ok?" I told him I was fine and that it actually felt better.

He told me to get up and walk around a little. "Just for a few minutes, so you don't get stiff." I went to the bathroom and then I walked around the living room and kitchen for a few minutes. He told me he was done with his homework and asked me if I would test him on some stuff. I perked up, "Yeah, sure I will." He gave me a list of questions and answers and I asked him the questions, one by one, and he answered them all right, except one. "Ask me again?" I asked him the questions in different order this time, and he got them all right and he was so proud of himself and I was proud of him too. This stuff looked and sounded hard, but he was a smart guy. He would make a wonderful Physician Assistant.

He told me that because he had the background as a Paramedic, it made it easier for him. He looked at me and said, "You should think about being a paramedic. They make between $40K - $70K a year and you make more with more education. Once I finish this course, I will get a raise. I am making $60K now and I will make $65K when I finish." He paused and then continued. "When I graduate this course, I can make the $70K, while I am waiting to find a job in my field. Once I do that, I will be making around $143K." I looked at him with wide eyes. "Are you fucking kidding me? OMG Sign me up." He laughed and said, "If you are serious, I will show you. It will cost you about $3,500 to take the course and you can get a student loan and pay it off when you finish. That is what I am doing and now I am attending University of New England online for this course. It's the cheapest one I could find, but you don't have to worry about that right now and you can just be a paramedic." I told him I was interested in becoming a paramedic and asked him if he would help me sign up for the student loan and for the course. He had the biggest smile on his face and said, "Abso-fucking-lutely." I told him that I thought about what he said about my parents and I was gonna call them tomorrow and I could tell them my plans for being a paramedic. "Maybe they would change their tune about me?" He tilted his head and said, "Aww, I hope so hon. I feel bad for you. There is nothing worse than not getting along with your parents and it's the same for the parents, you know?"

He got right on-line to Sallie Mae Student Loans and I signed up for the loan. He filled it all out for me, as I answered all their questions and he sent it off. He was talking to me about what he does and the course that he took and then he got a notification on his laptop. "There ya go. You are all set. You got approved. It only takes 15-20 minutes. It does help that you have really good credit." I looked shocked at him and said, "Already? I am approved? I got a student loan already?" He started laughing and said, "Yup, you are all set. You want to apply for the course now?" I was so shocked that all this was so fast. "YES, YES, I want to do this. How long will it take to do the course? Do I have to quit my job?" He smiled and said, "First you have to take the EMT course and then you take the Paramedic Course. The paramedic course is intense and takes between 1200-1800 hours and you can finish in 6 months to 2 years. The EMT course is 150 plus hours or you can take the Advanced EMT course, that will take you 150-300 hours. That is what I took and I think you should take that one because it will make it easier for you to take the paramedics course. I know this all sounds terrifying, because it was for me, but it went by fast and I put my mind to it."

He asked me if I had a laptop and I went to go get it in the bedroom. He entered the courses for me. The EMT Course is $1000.00 with a

$500 deposit and the balance is due within the first 2 weeks of class. He told me that it included the text book, stethoscope, blood pressure cuff, penlight, CPR certification and uniform polo shirt. Then I have to go for the National Registry testing and there is a fee for that too. Good thing I saved a lot of money. I chose the 6 week course, because Vinnie said that is what he did. I asked him, "Did you work while you took all these courses?" He told me he worked part time and his family helped him. I put my head down and said, "Well, that won't happen and I still have to pay rent here and eat, ya know, stuff like that?" He looked at me and said, "You can do this and I will help you. You will have to go to the training center labs too and I can take you, but that is all included in the tuition." I looked at him and said, "This is getting a little overwhelming. How can I do this and keep my job? I don't think my boss will let me work part-time. I signed on for the full-time position and if I go part-time, I may not be able to pay my rent." He said, "Don't get all nervous now. It will all work out. First off, you can still work full-time and maybe work something out with your boss to change your hours to coordinate with your classes and labs and explain what you are doing. He sounds like a nice guy from what you told me and I am sure he had the same problem at one point in his life. Let's just take it a moment at a time and don't get all nervous over it." I said ok, but I was still nervous. I needed that job to pay my rent. I had to pay half of $3,000 with Rain. She would be really pissed off, if I didn't pay the $1,500 towards it. I told him, "I could eat cereal, but I have pay my half of the rent" He laughed and said, "You will not eat cereal and you will pay your rent. Stop worrying about it."

He set everything up for me and I was so nervous about doing it. He signed me up for the later classes, so I could talk to my boss about coming in earlier or cutting my hours by 1-2 hours. I put my deposit on the course without even knowing if my boss would help me out. Vinnie looked at me and knew I was a nervous wreck. "Call your boss. Is he still there?" I looked at the clock and said, "He should be. Oh God." He said, "Why are you so nervous about this? There are still good people out there. All he can say is no and then we will go from there and figure something else out." I shook my head and dialed my boss. He answered and I froze. "Um. Graham?" He said, "Hey Renee, is everything ok? What happened at the chiropractor?" I told him that I had an adjustment and that I had to go back tomorrow and he told me to take the rest of the week off. "Graham, can I ask you a question?" He said, "Sure, shoot." I said, "This is hard for me." He interrupted me and said, "You are not quitting on me, are you?" I assured him that I had no plans of doing that and started explaining my situation. "Graham, I signed up to take an EMT course and then I want to become a paramedic after that, but I may need to adjust my hours, so I can do it. What do you think? Is that something I can do? I really need my job, so if it's not possible, just let me know." Graham shrieked and said, "OMG, Renee, that is fantastic. I think that is a wise move for you and I will help you in any way I can. You just let me know when you can work and we will adjust your hours here to anything you want. God, I am so proud of you." I was really shocked and said, "Really Graham? I can do that? Ohhh, Thank you so, so much. You have no idea how much this means to me. I want to take the course, but I also need my job so I can eat and pay my rent."

He was laughing in the background and said, "We have all been there. I have been there, so I know what you are going through. You just let me know what works for you because I don't want to lose you." I thanked him again and hung up. Vinnie smiled and said, "I TOLD YOU SO." I laughed at him and I felt better about taking the course. He touched my arm and said, "Now, you need to call your parents. TONIGHT." I must have had a scared look on my face and he said, "Nay, do you really think your parents could be mad at you for taking responsibility for your future? I don't. I think they would be proud as hell. I really do and I think they will be happy about it." I said, "Ok, Ok, I will do it." He replied and said, "Now Nay, right now." I looked at him and said, "Um." And he repeated himself. "Now Nay."

4

I picked up my phone and dialed. My mom picked up and said, "Nay? Is that you hon? OMG, I was so worried about you, but you left and you were mad, so I didn't want to call you and upset you anymore. Are you ok baby?" I told her I was fine. "Mom? How are you? Are you ok? I miss you mom. (I started crying) I'm sorry for everything I said. I am sorry." She told me that she was sorry too and I heard my Dad in the background " Tell her I'm sorry too." I told my mom to tell him I was sorry and now we got all that out of the way and everyone was sorry. Mom said, "Are you in trouble? Do you need help hon?" I told her, "Mom, I am fine. Rain and I have an apartment together and we both have a full time job. But I wanted to tell you something." There was silence and then she said, "Go Ahead hon. What do you want to tell me?" I said, "Well, I decided that I want to be a paramedic and I signed up for EMT classes first and then I will do the classes for paramedic. I may have to adjust my work hours, but I can do it. It's gonna take some extra time because I am working, but it's doable. What do you think?"

There was some whispering between her and my Dad, but I couldn't understand what they were saying. Finally, Mom got back on the phone and said, "Dad and I think that is fantastic and we are both very proud of you. We would like to help you out and pay your rent until you finish school. Will you let us do that?" Now I was silent. "Um, OMG, Mom, Dad, I love you both so much. It's a lot though. I pay $1,500 a month and I don't want you guys to be broke, but wow, that is a huge offer." Mom replied, "We put this money away to pay for your college, so we have it and we couldn't be more proud of you for this." I replied to her. "Thank you so much. This means a whole lot to me.

I have something else to tell you too. I met a guy and his name is Vinnie and he is a paramedic and he is studying to be a physician assistant. He is the one who told me all about this and (laugh) kinda talked me into it." Mom said, "Oh Honey, that is fantastic. I am happy you met someone like that."

Vinnie looked at me and whispered, "Tell her Nay." I sighed. "Mom, one more thing and I didn't want to tell you because you would have and probably still will say, 'I told you so'. She said, "What hon?." I told her the story how me and Rain went to the bar, blah, blah…. She was very concerned and said, "Are you all right now hon?" I told her that I had some neck and back and shoulder problems and my face was still a little black and blue, but Vinnie was taking care of me and I told her about the chiropractor and how we were meeting a lawyer tomorrow. She said, "Well at least you have someone there for you and Nay?" I said, "What mom?" She laughed and I heard my Dad laughing in the background. "We told you so." She was joking of course, but I knew she would say it. I spoke to my Dad briefly and then we hung up and I promised them that I would call them once a week and that if they needed anything to let me know and I thanked them for paying my rent.

Vinnie was smiling from ear to ear and said, "I told you so too. Didn't I say that everything would work out? Now, Graham will adjust your hours, so you can take your classes and even if you cut your hours, your rent will be paid for."

I was feeling so fucking happy for the first time in a long time. I had a great guy that cared about me, I had a full time job, I was talking to my parents again, I enrolled in some classes, I had a great boss and I was living in New York.

I got up from the table and walked over to Vinnie and planted one on him. "Thank you so much for making me do all of this. All of it. I wouldn't have, without you." He hugged me tight and I ended up sitting in his lap, which made him happy.

He picked me up and put me on the couch and got me the ice pack again. "It's time. Turn on your side and lean into the back of the couch." He was so attentive to me and my mom was even grateful that I had him. Everything in my life was turning around for the better, and I started thinking this was all a dream, after I got punched in the head, and I was going to wake up soon.

Vinnie stayed until about 11:30 and then went home and said he would see me in the morning with coffee and I told him that I would make him some breakfast. He pulled me close to him and said, "You are still *catching my eye.*

I know you feel what I feel. I know you do." I admitted it to him. I did feel something for him. I felt a lot of things for him and those feelings were getting stronger and stronger every day. He is always here for me, no matter what he has to do. He kissed me deep with an open mouth and his hot tongue was swishing inside and he was doing things to me and he knew it.

I said I wouldn't fall for the first guy I met, but I did and there is no going back now. He is the 'one'. I just know it in my heart. He left and I wanted him to stay, but I didn't want him to stay. Am I making any sense right now? Probably not, but he caught my heart and I caught his eye. I couldn't wait till tomorrow morning to see him again and touch him again and just be with him again.

I showered and got in my PJ's and took an ibuprofen and settled into bed. I actually slept pretty good, but when I got up, I was stiff as a board and my neck and back were killing me. I got up and got dressed, just in time, because my doorbell rang and it was Vinnie. He had our coffee's as promised. He kissed me as he came through the door and I apologized and told him I just got up. "I am so stiff today. Everything hurts on me, but I slept pretty good." He put the coffee's on the table and opened my fridge and took out butter, eggs and some precooked bacon and said, "I will do this, if you make toast." I said, "Oh, that is not why I said that, I can do it." He smiled and then bent over to kiss me and said, "I know that, but I will do it. Where are your pans and stuff." I pointed and then took the toaster out of the cabinet. He asked, "Is Rain here?" I laughed and said, "Let me go check, because I didn't hear her come home." I knocked on her door and she responded. "I am here and I would love some breakfast." And she laughed. She came out, wrapped up in her robe and went into the bathroom. Vinnie smiled and said, "Breakfast for 3." He got busy and made the eggs and I grabbed the bacon and made that in the microwave and put some toast down in the toaster.

We all sat down for breakfast and Rain said, "Thanks for making breakfast Vin. I usually just grab something on my way to work, so this is nice." He shook his head. We all caught up on each other's news and I told her that I registered for the EMT class and that Vinnie took me to the chiropractor and that we had an appointment with a lawyer today. She raised her eyebrows and said, "You are gonna sue the guy?" I shook my head and said, "Yeah and the bar too. I have pain in my neck, shoulder and back from falling." She shook her head and said, "Good for you and I think it's fantastic that you are taking a course and working too." I knew why she said that and I did not tell her I called my parents and that they were paying for my rent because that was none of her business. "Yeah, it will be a little overwhelming, but I can do it and Vinnie is gonna help me.

When I finish the EMT course, I am going for Paramedic." She looked at me and said, "Really? Wow, that's awesome Nay, that is really awesome. I wonder where you got that idea?" And she snickered under her breath. I looked at her and said, "Shut up Rain." She was just joking around and got up and patted me on the shoulder. "I wish you the best of everything girl. You know I do." She grabbed everyone's plate and rinsed them and put them in the dishwasher and I told her I would finish the rest. She saluted me and went in her bedroom.

I wasn't sure now, if she was really happy, if she was fooling around or what was going on. Rain was a hard person to figure out. I actually think she was a little jealous at this point, but I didn't care. Since we moved here, we haven't seen much of each other because I worked 8-4 and she worked 3-11, so she was gone when I got home and I was usually sleeping when she got home.

It was very seldom that we were home together or we got to go out together. The night that we went to the bar was one of those times, because she had a day off. It was the first time and probably the last time. I am beginning to see the attitude that my parents saw in her, but I failed to see. Maybe I am thinking too much about this. I will give her the benefit of the doubt.

Vinnie was sitting at the table and had his laptop out. He was checking when my classes start and said, "Ya got your money for the downpayment?" I got my purse out and gave him my credit card and he put it in, as I watched him. He handed it back and said, "You are all set. You start next week. YaHOO."

He got up and picked me up and turned me around in a circle. "You are gonna do great. I will help you. I changed my classes and my work hours." I pulled away and said, "WHAT? WHAT DID YOU DO VINNIE?" He started laughing. "Don't get upset. It's actually better for me. I can put more hours in this way. The other way I was only able to work 6 hours and now I can work 7-3 and put in 8 hours and our classes start at 4:00. We can eat supper together, if you want, and do our classes together, if you want. You can tell Graham you can work from 8-3 and you will only be losing an hour." I looked up at him and said, "Wow, you have this whole thing figured out, don't you?" He smiled a nervous smile at me and said, "Uh oh, Did I overstep my boundaries?" I smiled at him and said, "No, you didn't, but when did you do all this? You left late last night and got here early this morning." He said, "I texted my boss this morning and asked if I could switch shifts and he was happy about it, and told me he needed more people for the shift I wanted. And I switched my class just now. I guess I should have asked you before assuming everything."

He put his head down and said, "I'm sorry." I touched his cheek and said, "Don't be sorry. I am not mad at all, and thank you for caring so much about me and helping me." He looked down at me and said, "Next time I get one of my wild ideas, I will share with you and get your opinion first. I promise." I kissed those hot lips and said, "DEAL."

Rain was in her room for quite a while and didn't come out till 1:30 and just said, "Going to work." I told her to be careful and she shut the door and left.   Vinnie looked at me and said, "Can I ask you something?" I shook my head and he said, "Does she have a bug up her ass for some reason? She seems different from when I first met her, like something is bothering her." I laughed and said, "Now you know how Rain operates. I have noticed a lot more of her attitudes, since I moved in with her, and I think she is jealous or something. I think I am seeing what my parents saw that I didn't see at first." He said, "Even at breakfast, I wasn't sure if she was fooling around with you or she was mad that you were taking the course. I couldn't tell if she was happy about it, or mad about it." I laughed and said, "Yeah, I got the same feeling, but here's the thing, Vinnie, I don't give a shit what she thinks, because this is MY life, not hers and I am going to do what I think is right and I think this is right for me." He hugged me and said, "Good for you hon. You have the right attitude.

I had a friend that tried to talk me out of being an EMT and I told him to go fuck off." I laughed at him and he said, "He told me that we wouldn't be able to hang out like we did before and I told him, that I was an adult now and I needed a good future and hanging out with him was not in my future. Do you know where he is now? PRISON. That is where he ended up because he was hanging out with some asshole and they stole a car. And here I am with a beautiful woman who believes in me and loves me and I have a good job and I am still going to school to make myself better." I hugged him and said, "I DO believe in you Vinnie, and I am proud of you and I love you too."

5

I looked at the clock and said, "Shit, What time is my appointment with the lawyer?" He smiled and said, "3:30. We have time and you can go the way you are." It was 2:30 and I wanted to put on a little makeup but Vinnie told me not to put on any makeup so he could see my face and he said he had pictures he was going to give him. I said, "What is this lawyers name anyway?" He said, "Yeah you should probably know that huh? It's Attorney Art Castillo. He is a nice guy and he will do right by you."

We went to see Attorney Castillo, and on the way, Vinnie stopped to get us something to eat at a fast food place, because we didn't eat any lunch. We ate in the car and then headed to the attorney's office. It was a huge brick building, with lots of windows and stairs that went up to the two wooden front doors. The place was really big inside with elevators in the foyer. Vinnie stopped to look at the sign and said he was just making sure he was still on the second floor and he was. We took the elevator to the second floor and he pointed down the hall. We walked in and he went up to the receptionist and gave my name and I stood next to him. She said, "He will be ready for you in just a minute."

We sat down and he came out about 5 minutes later with a client that was leaving. "Vinnie, how are you Dude?" Vinnie stood up and shook his hand and then he introduced me and we walked into his office. He had me sign authorization forms to get my medical records and bills from The Mount Sinai Hospital and from Dr. Barclay. He spoke to both of us and got both stories. Vinnie sent him the pictures of my face that he took as he arrived on the scene and some from later in the hospital with my eye swollen shut and the big cut on my lip and corner of my mouth.

The attorney asked Vinnie to take another picture of me now and send it to him. So I stood up and Vinnie took it and sent it to him. "Ok Renee, You are all set. We will be building your case with your future medical bills and records, and any missed time from work. It doesn't matter if you were paid or not" I gave him the dates, including this week and we left. We were only there for about 45 minutes.

Vinnie turned to me in the elevator and said, "Do you like him?" I shook my head yes. He continued, "He is very thorough and won't miss a thing. He will get you as much money as possible." I said, "Vinnie, how do you know him? What did you go to him for?" He laughed a little and said, "I got bit by a dog when I went to a house for an emergency call. I will show you my scar later. It was really bad and Gary had to bandage me up before we left the house." I said, "OMG, really? How awful. Did the owner have to put the dog down?"

He told me that he asked that the dog NOT be put down, because he was just protecting his owner, who had a heart attack and couldn't put the dog away before we got there. But he said, "I sued the owner for just my medical bills and lost time from work and his insurance paid for it. The owner was so thankful that I didn't want the dog put down. I would never do that, because it's just plain mean. I could see if the dog was actually mean, but he was just doing his job. I rubbed his shoulder as he was driving. "You did a good thing Vinnie."

We got back to my place and he told me that he brought his notes from when he took the EMT course and wanted to know if I wanted to look at them and that I could keep them if I wanted. My eyes lit up and I said, "Really? Yes, I would love to take a peek and see what I am in for. It will let me know how scared I should be." He started laughing and said, "I know you are a smart girl and you will do just fine."

He opened the trunk and took out a notebook and he carried it upstairs to my apartment. He set me up on the couch with the notebook and an ice pack and I skimmed through them first and from what I saw, I didn't think it would be too hard. He watched TV while I was going through them and he told me to ask him any questions I had. I was really interested in his notes. He was very thorough in his note taking and he had a very neat hand writing and he knew how to spell and I read page after page. I actually had a hard time putting it down. It was like a good book and had me sitting on the edge of my seat, waiting for the climax.

I kept looking at him every now and then, wondering how I was so lucky to meet him and how smart he was. You could tell by the notes he took, how smart he was. He didn't miss anything.

He was watching a movie about a detective that got in with the wrong crowd of people. He looked down at me and said, "What do you think so far?" I looked up at him and said, "I can't put it down. It's so interesting and I am gonna love this." He smiled at me, kissed my forehead and said, "I told you so."

I asked him, "Where is your dog bite scar? I don't need to see it if you have to take your pants off." He laughed and took off his left boot and pulled up his jeans and showed me the huge scar on his shin bone. It was about 6 inches long and jagged. I said, "Oh my God, Vinnie. That is so bad. How come it is so big?" He said, "The dog wouldn't let go and I was pulling away and he ripped my skin and it made it bigger, but the pain was so bad and I kept trying to get away from him. Gary was able to remove him and he put him in another room and closed the door, while I screamed like a baby. You can't imagine how bad it hurt and there was blood everywhere. Gary cut my uniform and had to pour alcohol on it and I screamed so loud, I am surprised you didn't hear me in Delaware. He had to stop the bleeding and bandage me up, so he called for backup to help the actual patient. It really was a blood bath." I just looked at him in shock. I said, "HOLY SHIT Vinnie. That must have been horrible, just horrible." He said, "It was and I don't like dogs now. Don't ever ask for one. I will, however, have cats." He laughed, but he was serious and after hearing that story, and seeing that scar, I don't want a dog either.

The next morning, I called Graham and told him that I could work 8-3 and he was so happy and said, "That is wonderful and I can work with that. How are you feeling?" I told him that I had another chiropractor appointment that afternoon and I was feeling a bit better. I told him I was using ice packs and resting.

Vinnie came with coffee and breakfast for just me and him and we sat at the kitchen table talking when Rain emerged from her bedroom and I could tell she had an attitude already. "Hey Rain, how's work going?" She just leaned on the counter in the kitchen waiting for her coffee to brew in the Keurig and said, "It's ok, I am so tired. I think I am gonna take the day off. What are you two doing today?" I told her I had a chiropractor appointment today but we were just gonna hang around.

Vinnie didn't say a word to her and I could tell he didn't like her. She pulled a chair out at the table and put her coffee down on the table and bent over and sipped it without picking it up. I laughed and said, "You are that tired that you can't pick up the cup?" She gave me the dirtiest look and I thought she was gonna slap me. I looked at her and said, "I was joking Rain. You gotta bug up your ass?" She took her cup and went in her bedroom and didn't say a fucking word to me.

I looked at Vinnie and he was staring at me. He whispered, "*What the fuck is wrong with her*?" I thought I heard her crying, so I got up and listened at her door. She was crying, so I knocked and opened the door. I went in her room and closed the door. "What's wrong Rain? I never saw you like this. I was only joking with you, like I always do. I would never say anything to hurt you. Talk to me." She looked at me and said, "I'm sorry Nay. I am so upset. I see you with Vinnie and my dream is coming to an end. You will move out with him and I will be stuck with this place all by myself and I will have to move out." I looked shocked at her and said, "Do you really think I would do that to you? For real Rain? Come on. You know me better than that. I would never ever move out on you and stick you with this place. You forgot that this was OUR dream, not just yours. Actually, I have news for you…I called my parents and told them I was taking on-line courses and they will be paying my rent for as long as it takes me to finish and become a paramedic." She looked up at me and said, "You called them? You did? Maybe I should call my parents too. I feel so bad for the way I left and for the things I said. I am so sorry for acting this way. I don't know what's gotten into me."

I rubbed her shoulder and said, "Call them. You are their daughter and they were just words. I am sure they are worrying about you. They will forgive you and I am sure they feel bad and they miss you. I think you miss them too." She started crying. "What am I gonna do without you Nay?" I told her I wasn't going anywhere yet and when I finally do want to move out, it won't be a surprise and it will be a planned move and she would have plenty of notice. She hugged me and said, "You are right, I am jealous. I wish I could find a guy like Vinnie. He is so nice and he is so good to you." I said, "Your guy is out there, you will find him, or he will find you, when the time is right. I guarantee it." She thanked me for coming in to find out what was wrong and I left and went back out to Vinnie.

Vinnie looked up at me as I came out of her bedroom. "Everything ok?" I shook my head yes and whispered to him that I would tell him everything later. He whispered, *"It's not me, is it?"* I laughed and said, "No, absolutely not. Do you remember what time my chiropractor appointment is?" He said, "Yeah, I have your appointment card right here." He pulled it out of his wallet and said, "2:30." I acknowledged him by shaking my head. "I should take a shower and put something decent on." He said, "If I were you, I wouldn't take a shower, because he uses that goopy stuff for the laser treatment and it gets sticky. You should wait till you get home. You can do what you want, it's just a suggestion."

I smiled at him and said, "Ok, suggestion taken. I will just change my clothes then." We still had about 4 hours and I wanted to look at his notes again. I went in the living room to get them and brought them into the kitchen and opened it to where I left off last night. He smiled and showed me his friggin white teeth and his eyes were sparkling at me. "I am so happy you are this interested." I told him that his notes were like a good book and he laughed at me. "I can't wait to start. Monday at 4?" He said, "Yup, me too. You want me here? It's ok if you don't." I gave him a puzzled look. "What do you mean? I thought you were gonna be with me and you were gonna take your classes with me? And we were gonna eat dinner together?" He said, "That was the plan, but I don't want to assume like I did in the past, so I am just asking you." I smiled at him and said, "Well, thanks for checking in with me. I want you here with me and I want to eat dinner together and take our classes together." He touched my hand from across the table and said, "Thanks, I am really looking forward to this."

I said, "Well, eating out can be expensive, so what do you say we pick out some recipes, go shopping for the ingredients and then prep on the weekends, so when we get home from work, we can finish it up quick and eat?" He said, "I don't really know how to make anything except eggs, toast, bacon and sausage, but I'm in." I laughed and said, "If you can make that, then you can help prep and I will teach you how". He said, "Ok, well, we can split the bill for the groceries, so you are not footing the bill for that." I agreed. I got my recipe book off the book shelf and we went through the whole thing and we put post-its on the ones we thought would be good. I had family recipes written on notebook paper stuck in between the recipes and he was looking at them. "Mom's recipes?" I shook my head and told him they were all excellent.

He took all of them out of the book and put them on the table next to his laptop. He said, "I am gonna type them all out for you and print them. When we go shopping, I will pick you up a 3-ring binder with sleeve covers and you can put them in there to save them. They will get ruined the way they are." I was shocked. "Really? You are gonna type them all?" He shook his head and said, "In a couple years, you won't even be able to read this. It has to be done to save them."

He started typing them and he sent me the recipes, as he finished each one, on my computer to look over, against the written recipes to check and make sure he had all the ingredients and directions correct. This guy was unbelievable. Where the hell did he come from? He is typing my mom's recipes? Jeez. I couldn't wait to tell my mom about this. He was a fast typer too. I did a lot of typing in high school and I was pretty good too. I had him send me the form he was using and I dug in and started typing some myself. We finished in no time and we printed them out.

I looked at the clock and it was 12:30. "Hey, you want me to make some sandwiches for lunch?" He shook his head and said, "Yeah, that would be great." I boiled some eggs and made an egg salad and got my Wavy Lays out of the pantry and grabbed a couple of waters. He thanked me and kept looking at me and I said, "What?" He whispered, "*Can I ask you something*?" I shook my head and he whispered, "*Who buys the groceries here? You? Or do you split the cost with Rain?*" I laughed and whispered back, "*Well, she owes me some money because I have been doing all the shopping and she said that she doesn't eat much. I know it's all a bunch of bullshit and she is taking me for a ride, but I will get it from her.*" He raised his eyebrows and continued to whisper, "*She is taking advantage of you Nay. How much does she owe you, if you don't mind me asking?*" I whispered to him that she owed me a couple of hundred dollars. I told him, that I would cook and then she would eat the leftovers the day after or when she got home from work. He whispered, "*Yeah, that must be nice. Just like home. Mommy cooks and you eat for free. That is not right. Sorry, but she needs to come up with the money or there will be no more leftovers. I will eat them.*" And he laughed. I wasn't sure if Rain was sleeping or eavesdropping on our conversations, so we whispered when we talked about her.

I cleaned up lunch and we left to go to the chiropractor. On the way, Vinnie was still thinking about Rain and how she was using me. He said, "I wonder how long she thinks she can get away with this shit of not paying you for her food?" I laughed. "Not much longer. I will leave her a post-it note with the amount on the fridge and see what happens. I will keep you posted." He laughed and said,

"Good, don't forget Nay, because she will use you as long as she can, unless you say something," I told him I had all the receipts and I would put them on the fridge under the magnets so she could see them.

We met with the chiropractor and he used the laser or whatever it was called on my neck, shoulder and back. He used a Tens Unit and then adjusted my mid-back again. Vinnie told him that he was putting ice packs on it regularly. He told me to make another appointment for next week and I told him that was impossible because I had to go back to work and then I had classes, so he told me to come back on Friday this week and he also said he was open on Saturday mornings and to make one for next week on Saturday. Vinnie went to the front desk and got my appointments while he was finishing up my treatments.

We headed back to my apartment and we picked out some recipes and wrote down the ingredients and made a list of what we needed. I knocked on Rain's door and there was no answer, so I knocked again and just opened the door. She wasn't home. I put the receipts on the fridge door along with the amount she owed me and Vinnie smiled at me. We took off for the grocery store and he helped me grab the stuff we needed. We got stuff for tonight and tomorrow night too. I tried to pick some casseroles and one pan meals to make it easier. Vinnie said he would take me out on Saturday and Sunday.

I got stuff for my lunches and he got stuff for his too, while we were there. We got the 3-ring binder for the recipes too. We got home and put the groceries away and then he wanted me to put ice on my back for 20 minutes. While I was doing the ice, he put all the recipes in the binder for me and put it back on my bookshelf.

Then we got busy preparing supper for tonight. He sat at the counter in one of the high counter chairs and said, "What do you want me to do?" I gave him a pepper and an onion and told him to dice and slice them. He looked up at me and said, "How?" I showed him quick, so he knew what I meant and he did a great job. He smiled and said, "This is my first slice and dice job." I laughed at him and said, "It won't be your last either." We prepared dinner for that night, which was sausage and pepper grinders, and he was impressed and said it was delicious. We did the same for the rest of the week and went out to eat for dinner on Saturday and Sunday. I saw the chiropractor on Friday and he said, I was doing so much better and I told him it felt good. He wanted to see me next Saturday and then he would evaluate me.

During the day on Saturday and Sunday, we prepared meals for the week, so we could eat before or during our classes. We made a taco casserole, which was easy and I got some Grands rolls, which only take a few minutes in the air fryer. We made a chicken and rice casserole and baked it, so all we had to do was warm it up. I made a baked ziti and baked that too. And we decided that we would have pancakes and bacon one night and then we would have all the leftovers and we were done. Vinnie said, "I really enjoyed cooking with you and this was a really good idea. It will save a lot of money during the week".

The post-it note and the receipts disappeared from the fridge and Rain put $300.00 on the fridge under the magnet.   I took it and put a $50 back because her bill was $250.00. The $50 stayed there for over a week, so I took it down and put it on her dresser with a note. She put it back on the fridge and told me to keep it for the food she was eating, so I took it. She was eating leftovers from what we cooked, so that was her share. Vinnie was actually shocked that she paid me, but I wasn't. I knew she wouldn't do that to me.

So Monday was here and I was so excited. I went to work at 8 and got out at 3:00 and rushed home to heat up dinner and Vinnie got here at 3:20 and eager to get going. It was an early dinner, but we got used to it and we ended up eating snacks later. Sometimes, we weren't hungry, so we ate after classes. He set up the laptops on the kitchen table with our notebooks for taking notes and pens and pencils and earbuds for each of us. I heated up dinner and we sat and ate together. I cleared the dishes and he helped to load the dishwasher and he put the casserole back in the fridge. We were ready. I was ready! We got on-line and waited till the classes started.

It seemed to go by so fast and was very interesting. Vinnie was deep into note writing and staring at his screen. He had an extra half hour more than me, so I cleaned up and put some ice on my back in the living room while he finished up.

***

I was done with my chiropractic treatments and I was much better and I would just go for maintenance once a month. I finished my EMT classes and also my paramedic classes and continued my job as a pharmacy technician until I was hired by Vinnie's boss. Graham was happy for me and told me how much he appreciated that I stayed while taking the classes and congratulated me. Vinnie was still taking his classes for physician's assistant and he was only half way through.

6

My parents were so proud of me and wanted to know when I was coming to visit. I told them that I was going to take 2 weeks vacation before starting my new job as paramedic and asked if I could visit and bring Vinnie and they said yes. I couldn't wait for them to meet him. He was excited to meet them as well. Rain finally called her parents and she went to visit them the same week we went.

My mom and dad loved Vinnie and he was part of the family from the moment he walked through the front door. My mom and dad were over the hill happy that I graduated and I was now a paramedic and they thanked Vinnie for talking me into it. Mom handed me an envelope that had the rest of my college fund in it and I told her to keep it, because I may want to continue my education and become a physician assistant. I hadn't said anything to Vinnie and he looked at me when I said that and opened his mouth in surprise. "Really? Really? That is awesome." He came to hug me and picked me up and twirled me around.

I told him that I really liked the field and wanted to continue. My mom and dad were shocked too and they came to hug me too.

Vinnie and I slept in separate rooms during our visit and I think my mom and dad were a little surprised. I told my mom later that we have not been intimate yet and that I wanted to wait.

Vinnie and I spent 4 days with them and I showed him around my hometown and we went out to eat and to the movies and my mom and dad made a nice dinner and we took them out to dinner. We all had a really nice time together. I am so grateful that Vinnie made me call them or I wouldn't be doing this with them and I think the longer it took me to do it, the worse it would have been.

We had a nice drive back to New York and took some time to enjoy our vacation time. We went to the mall and did some shopping, and we ate out and went to the movies and did some mini-golf and even went back to the bar where I was punched. We sat towards the back of the room and we just had a few drinks and then left. I was a little nervous to be there, but Vinnie said I would be fine and, of course, I was.

Vinnie and I have been together for a little more than 3 months now and he was getting pretty frisky when we watched TV at night. I think I made him wait long enough. Actually, I couldn't wait anymore. He was turning me on, over and over, and I couldn't hold back another minute and before you know it, I was all over him and I think I surprised him. He went right along with me, as I knew he would, and we really got hot and heavy and transferred from the couch to the bed. He kissed me everywhere… and I did the same… and we rolled around for what seemed like hours and we enjoyed each other. There was no more waiting and we became one!! We fell asleep like we were and he spent his first night with me. I woke up in the middle of the night and he had covered me with the comforter and tucked me in around my body. He had his arm around me and he held me for the rest of the night. It was the best vacation, ever. And we repeated that night, every single night and I couldn't have been happier.

Before our vacation was over, we visited Attorney Castillo and got my suit filed with the Court, because I was done treating and he had all my medical bills.

Our vacation was over and it was my first day. I was working first shift with Vinnie and that made me really happy, because he was my support team. The first day is very nerve racking, even though I was sure of myself in what I learned and I was positive I could handle anything that came along. Our first call was a really bad car accident. It was two cars that hit head-on. I got right in and did my job, and I even tolerated all the blood, and there was a lot of it. Vinnie was proud of me and I was proud of me. I think that was the only thing I was afraid of and I just passed the test. It's the best thing in the world, to know that you helped someone or saved someone's life. Vinnie said, the big test was seeing a dead body that was mangled. He said, he still has a hard time with it, especially when it is a young kid and he said he almost quit when he saw his first baby. He needed therapy after that one. I started to panic after he told me that and dreaded when that day came.

Months and months went by and we were still working together, studying together, cooking together and sleeping together. I was really happy with him. He never complained about anything. He always treated me with kid gloves and cared for me and protected me.

He had 3 months to go before he graduated and he had to do a few weeks of labs, so we didn't get to be together every night, but we were during the day and after his labs ended at 8:00 p.m.

Rain was still being her bitchy self. She had her moments when she was nice, but most of the time, she was unhappy about something or other or complaining or depressed over something. She had a boyfriend now and I wondered how he put up with her attitude all the time. I don't think he will be around much longer, because she is so mean to him and I really don't think she likes him. Is she just keeping him around and using him for free dinners and sex? I really don't get this girl.

She needs to grow up. He was a nice guy and he was super friendly and sweet to her. He was always buying her flowers and little presents and she was so unappreciative. I was just waiting for the day that she came home crying and telling us that he broke up with her. It will be hard for me, not to tell her off. Vinnie is waiting too. He stares at them while we are studying and they are in the kitchen. Rain quit her job and decided to take my job with Graham. She had to do the training first, but Graham said she was working out. So now, she worked 8-4 everyday and she was home when we were home. *UNCOMFORTABLE.* Vinnie and I were used to being alone at dinner and for studying. A couple times, they were loud and fooling around in the kitchen, so we picked up our stuff and went to Vinnie's place. They apologized, but we needed to study. We were serious about what we were doing.

Vinnie wanted me to move in with him, so I talked to Rain to see where she was with her boyfriend and asked her if she was ready to move. She opened her mouth in horror. "What? You are gonna move out on me. I thought we had a deal that you would give me time and all that?" I told her to calm down. "Um, That is what I am doing right now. I didn't say I was moving out tomorrow Rain. I said that Vinnie asked me to move in and now I am discussing this with you. It won't be immediately and you will have plenty of time to look for another apartment. What about Jason? Does he want you to move in with him?" She looked like I killed her and she was about to fall over. I almost laughed in her face, but she was so serious. "Seriously Rain? I told you I wasn't going to be here forever. I have a few more months to go, to finish this course and I would like to be out of here by then. That gives you plenty of time." As usual, I was the bad guy and everything was all my fault. She turned around with her back to me and crossed her arms. Oh, here it comes, the Kindergarten temper tantrum. She better not start with me because I have had enough of her shit, living here with her. I just stood there with MY arms crossed looking at her back and then I walked away and while I was walking I said, "I could just say, Bye, I am moving this weekend and not give you any notice and if you keep up this Kindergarten shit, that's what's gonna happen. I am sick of this crap." She flipped around and said, "NO, don't do that to me. I am sorry." I had fire in my eyes when I looked at her and said, "I am tired of your temper tantrums Rain. Grow up already. It's time. You are 22. You are an adult, so act like one. I am giving you 2 months notice now and then I am out."

She started crying and said, "What happened to 3 months notice?" I told her she lost one because of her tantrum and if she keeps it up, it will be tomorrow. "I promise you Rain, you don't want me to tell you what I really think right now, so just LEAVE ME ALONE and let it go." But NO, she couldn't leave it alone, so I let her have it.

 "YOU DON'T BUY GROCERIES AND HAVE NEVER EVER GONE GROCERY SHOPPING ONE TIME, EITHER WITH ME OR BY YOURSELF, BUT YOU EAT THE MEALS I MAKE AND YOU COMPLAIN ABOUT THEM TOO!! YOU DON'T CLEAN, YOU DON'T COOK, AND I DO YOUR FUCKING LAUNDRY. EVERYTHING I DO BOTHERS YOU. YOU ARE JEALOUS OF VINNIE AND YOU ARE RUDE TO HIM. YOU ARE MEAN TO YOUR OWN BOYFRIEND AND HE IS SUPER SWEET TO YOU. I COULD GO ON AND ON AND I PROMISE YOU, YOU DON'T WANT TO HEAR ANYMORE. YOU KEEP IT UP AND YOU WON'T HAVE ONE FRIEND LEFT. I AM DONE RAIN. DONE. DONE. I WILL BE MOVING OUT THIS WEEKEND. I TRIED TO BE NICE. I WISH YOU LUCK!!

She was crying hard now and I had not one shred of empathy for her. She pushed the wrong button.

I texted Vinnie and asked if he had any boxes. He was in his lab at school, so he didn't answer right away, but when he did he said, "Uh oh. Didn't go well?" I just texted him back and said, "Nope, I need boxes. Moving this weekend, if that is ok" He told me it was fine with him and he had some flattened boxes in his garage and he would grab some packing tape to put them back together. Vinnie had a house and I was really looking forward to moving in with him.

I went in my bedroom and slammed the door, so she knew better than to come and talk to me anymore tonight. I emptied my dresser and just left a couple of outfits on top to wear for Friday and Saturday morning. I piled everything on a shelf in the closet. We had a furnished apartment, so I had my clothes, personal stuff and the pots and pans were mine and the dishes, silverware and baking pans were all mine.

She put nothing into this apartment except her body. I went in the living room and took my trinkets off the shelf and a pillow off the couch. I took all the spices and canned goods. Basically, everything was mine because I bought it and she paid me nothing. The only time she paid me was when I left the post-it note on the fridge. It was like pulling teeth and I was totally done living here with her.

Vinnie was right about her. She was a USER. I emptied everything and Vinnie helped me pack it when he got home, and he taped everything and labeled it. She stayed in her bedroom crying and I still felt nothing. I guess she pushed me to my limit, because I was a caring person and always had empathy for everyone. This is how I knew I was done with her.

Jason came to the door while we were packing and he whispered to me, *"What happened?"* I whispered back, *"Your girlfriend is an asshole. I am moving out on Saturday. Good luck with her."* He was shocked and said, *"Oh my God. What is she gonna do now?"* I said, *"Oh, I don't know and I don't care. Maybe you could move in with her?"*

Vinnie was smirking while packing the silverware. Jason patted me on the shoulder and he pointed to her bedroom door and I shook my head that she was in there. He knocked and no answer so he opened up her door and she was on her bed crying. He closed the door behind him and there was a lot of muffled talking. I really didn't give a shit what they were saying because I was so fucking pissed at her. I don't think I have ever been this pissed at anyone. Vinnie came up behind me and he knew I was really upset. He hugged me from behind and whispered in my ear, *"Don't let her get to you. She is a user and I wouldn't be surprised if Jason came out and said they were through. I wouldn't want her. She is such a little baby and if things don't go her way, she stamps her feet like a toddler."* I told him I was actually fine. Mad, but fine.

We continued to pack up the kitchen till everything was empty. I looked at Vinnie and said, "And I am taking everything in the fridge and freezer too because I paid for it." And I wasn't whispering and I didn't care if she heard me. We packed up my closet and all the stuff I took out of my dresser and I went in the bathroom and took all my towels, toothpaste, toothbrush, the liquid shower gel, the shampoo, the conditioner, my shower cap, my sponge, deodorant, makeup and my razor. I took everything out of the medicine cabinet too. It was all mine and I paid for it.

The more I packed, the more I was angry with her because it became apparent to me that she really did use me and everything in that apartment was mine. I even took all the fucking toilet paper. Good Luck asshole!

Vinnie was watching me in the doorway and said, "What if I have to take a shit?" He busted out laughing. I had to laugh because he made me do it. I left a 1/4 inch on the roll that was hanging there and pointed to it and said, "Is that enough?". He said, "Seeing as you packed everything, I might as well pack up the car and we can take it all over to my house now. Why wait till Saturday?" We both carried boxes down, one by one and emptied the whole apartment. He said, "You might as well take the comforter and sheets and pillows and stay with me tonight." So I stripped my bed and folded everything up and put it into a trash bag and he carried the trash bag down to his car. We still had more boxes and he said we should make a couple of trips and get it all out before she took stuff out. All the boxes were sealed, so we would know if she did. We made 2 more trips and we were done. I didn't even say goodbye or leave her a note. I was GONE. I contacted the landlord on my way to Vinnie's house and told him that I was moving out and it would be up to Rain to make the payments. Our lease was done, so I owed nothing and I told him she could have the security deposit. That was mine too. He appreciated the call to let him know.

Vinnie and I were up till after midnight putting my clothes and things away. I added my shower stuff to his shower and he needed dishes, silverware and stuff, so I just added my things to his. We broke the boxes apart and he stacked them in his garage.

We only had a handful of boxes left and we were done. It actually worked out for both of us that I moved out tonight, because I didn't have a class and he just finished his labs. I told him I wanted to take a day off, but I didn't have any vacation time accrued yet, so he told me to call in sick and he would too. "We can say that we both ate something bad." He laughed and made believe he had to run to the bathroom to take a shit and he was holding his ass. He always made me laugh and brought me out of my moods. I very rarely got into a mood, but he was right there, if I did.

We ended up calling in sick and it worked. We slept in till 10:00 and our boss called and wanted to know what happened and Vinnie told him, "Oh My God, Don't eat at The Garden. Jeez, we were fighting over the bathroom all night. It was really bad and now we just have upset stomachs." He told us to both feel better and he hung up. I started laughing and said, "It worked, but now, the poor Garden isn't gonna get too many customers." He laughed and said, "He probably won't say anything to anyone."

We wanted to go out for breakfast, but we didn't want to be seen by anyone, so I offered to make breakfast at home. I made some pancakes and sausage and Vinnie made a couple cups of coffee and we sat at his big kitchen table. I said, "Are you renting this house furnished?" I asked because the furniture in this place looked expensive.

He smiled at me and said, "I bought the house and this is all my own furniture. Some of it came with the house because the previous owners didn't want it, so I lucked out there." I looked up at him and said, "You own it? Wow, I thought you rented it. That's awesome Vinnie. I am so proud of you." I paused for a minute and then said, "I would like to help you pay your mortgage, now that I am living here and we can still split the groceries. Is that something you would agree to?" He looked at me wide eyed and said, "I wish I could say no, but I would love the help and actually, your rent would be half of what you were paying now. My mortgage is $1,500, so if you could give me $750 a month and we split the groceries, that would be great. I will pay for everything else, like gas and electric and I love you for offering." I went to shake hands with him and say 'deal' and he picked me up and hugged me tight and kissed me. I offered to pay for all the groceries, because my mom and dad were still giving me $1,500 for rent money every month from my college fund. "If you are paying for electric and gas, then I can pay for all the groceries. What do you say?" He was hesitating, but I knew he needed help. "Please

let me Vinnie!". He smiled and shook his head
yes. "Thank you so much Nay. This helps me
so much, but I reserve the right to take you out
to eat on the weekends and anything else we
do on the weekends ok?" I agreed. He said,
"I knew it was gonna be hard for me to do this
on my own and I tried to rent it, but they
wanted to sell it, so I went out on a limb and
bought it. It's been a little tough, but I am
making it." I told him that I would help him as
much as I could and we would eat good
meals.

7

My phone was ringing. I looked at it and it was Rain. I looked at Vinnie and said, "It's Rain, should I answer it?" He shrugged his shoulders. I picked it up and answered. "It's me, Rain, don't hang up Nay. I am so so sorry. I know I was acting like an asshole. I know you won't come back, but I still want to be friends with you and I am sorry for the way I acted. Can you forgive me Nay?" I didn't say anything for a few moments and then remembered how fucking mad she made me. "What do you want Rain?" She started crying and said, "I don't want anything. I just want you to be my friend and I called to apologize to you. Will you forgive me?" I said, "Yeah, ok, whatever." She was crying and said, "I don't know what I am going to do, Nay. Jason left me and I thought maybe he would move in with me or he would ask me to move in with him, but he left and now I have no one."

I rolled my eyes and let her have it. "Well, Rain, you did this to yourself. You were so mean to him. You can't treat people like that and expect them to hang around, so you can keep doing it. Why do you think I left Rain? Do you know how mad you made me? I tried to talk to you about moving out and I originally gave you 3 months to find another place. I had no plans on leaving last night and if you weren't able to find a place in 3 months, do you think I would have left you flat? NO, I WOULDN'T HAVE. I would have given you more time, but you pushed my buttons and pushed my buttons and then you pushed the wrong button. I am not gonna stay there and put up with your Kindergarten shenanigans and temper tantrums. My parents were right about you."

She was still crying during my rant and said, "What am I supposed to do now though?" I said, "OH, I don't know, maybe you should call mommy and daddy and go home, where they can buy your groceries and make you dinner and do your laundry?" She slammed the phone down and then hung up. Vinnie was snickering with his hand over his mouth. He said, "Oh MY GOD, Nay, you are really mad at her huh? I can't believe you just said all that to her." I was taking some deep breaths to calm down because, as usual, she pissed me off again. He said, "You ok hon?" I shook my head yes, but I was out of breath and I thought I was having some kind of panic attack. He was rubbing my back and had me lay down on the couch and he put an ice pack on my forehead to snap me out of it. I was ok after a few minutes. I said, "I can't talk to her anymore. She pissed me off so much that she is giving me panic attacks. I am done with her. I mean really done. I am not answering her calls anymore." He looked at me and said, "Just block her Nay and be done with it." He handed me my phone and I blocked her. "SON OF A BITCH. How the hell does she get under my skin so easy?" He put his arm around me and said, "Forget about her and calm down. She expects you to forgive her and come to her rescue again."

We ended up unpacking the last of the boxes into the afternoon and straightening everything out and I did an Instacart grocery order. I got a rotisserie chicken, some fresh broccoli, instant mashed potatoes and brown gravy mix and that is what we ate that night. I ordered stuff for the rest of the week, plus lunchmeat and rolls and stuff for our lunches. Vinnie and I went through the recipes that we picked out earlier, with the post-it notes attached to them and I got all the ingredients that we needed. He helped me do the prepping, chopping and sauté and we had everything ready to go. We got along so well. We never even had a disagreement. I hope it stays this way or I will have to find another place to live and I really don't want to. I loved him and I loved my job, I loved living with him and I was happy.

Our first week living together at Vinnie's, was awesome. We worked together during the day, we cooked together every night, and we did our classes together every night. Saturday and Sunday, he took me out to eat for dinner, but we still made breakfast and lunch at home.

We were trying to save up some money for a small vacation and have some in reserve for emergencies. It was easier for me because my mom and dad sent me $1,500 every month, so I didn't have to touch my paycheck at all. Vinnie said it was so much easier for him, now that I was living there because I paid for half of the mortgage and for all of the groceries, so he had money to save too.

8

A few months had passed and I got a call from Rain's parents. I picked up the phone and I heard her mom crying. "Renee? Hi, it's Mary, Rain's mom. How are you honey?" I loved her mom and dad. They were so down to earth and friendly. "Hi Mary, how are you? What's wrong?" She paused before she answered and I heard her blow her nose. "I just called to tell you that Rain is in Rehab." I had a puzzled look on my face. "Rehab for what Mary?" She started to cry again and said, "She almost overdosed on drugs after you left her in the apartment. Her boyfriend went to the apartment to check on her, because she wasn't answering her phone and found her almost dead." I was shocked. "WHAT? What are you talking about? Rain didn't do drugs. I know that for a fact Mary. I lived with her."

Mary said, "Well, she did after you left because she was so upset." I rolled my eyes, because I knew that Rain lied to her mom about what happened so I said, "Well, I am not sure about what she told you Mary, but this is what really happened. I told her that I would give her 3 months notice, before I was going to move out so she would have time to find a new roommate, or find a new apartment. She was acting out and having a temper tantrum and she got into my face, so I moved out that night. I want you to know that I paid for everything in that apartment. I did the grocery shopping, I did all the cooking, I did all the cleaning and I even did her fucking laundry. She used me for everything, Mary, but I put up with it. When she started giving me a hard time, I just packed up and left. She was making me get panic attacks. She was mean to me and mean to my boyfriend and she was mean to Jason too. I don't know what got into her." Mary said, "What got into her was drugs, Nay. That is what got into her. You didn't know she was using?" I said, "WHAT, NOOO. NOOO, She couldn't have. I think I would know. REALLY? All this time, she was using and I didn't know?" Mary said, "Yes, she was. The doctor said she had been using for a long time, probably even before she moved to New York." I couldn't believe what I was hearing. I said, "Oh, Mary, I am so sorry. I wish I knew about it, but I had no idea. How is she doing in Rehab?" Mary started crying again and said, "I don't think she is gonna make it, Nay.

She was mean to us and won't talk to us and I
know when she gets out, she will start all over
again." I really didn't know what to say to her
and now I wasn't sure why she really called
me. I was not going to get involved with this.
NOPE, not doing it. Mary started talking
again, "Do you think you can talk to her and
have her call us? We keep calling her and she
won't answer and she won't return our calls."
There it was, the reason she actually called. I
was sticking to my guns and not getting
involved. "Well, Mary, I am sorry, but I am not
going to get involved with your family matters.
I am sorry you are going through this. I really
am, but I am not calling her."

Mary said, "Please Nay, please call her and tell
her to call me. I don't want to lose my
daughter." I said, "Mary, I don't want you to
lose your daughter, but there is nothing I can
do or say to change her mind about what she
is doing to herself. Just keep calling her and
sooner or later, she will break down and talk to
you. It will happen. I am sorry, but I am not
getting involved with this. I am going to
school and I am working a full time job. I don't
have the energy to deal with this right now."

Mary hung up on me. Gee, that was nice. Now I know where her daughter got it from.

I called my mom and told her what just happened and she was shocked too that Rain was on drugs. Mom said, "Did Mary say what kind of drugs she was on?" I told her that she never said what kind, but she made it sound like I caused her overdose because I left her at the apartment after the fight. She made me believe that this was all my fault. My mom told me not to worry about her or Mary. "They are both fucking users Nay and you can see that right?" I told her I can definitely see that both of them were. I never talked to Mary, so I knew she had a reason for calling me and of course, she did and when I wouldn't help her and she didn't get her way, she hung up. Mom asked me how school was going and she asked how Vinnie was and I told her we were still attending school and doing good. She told me how proud she was of me and that made me feel so good.

Vinnie was at one of his labs tonight, but I texted him and told him what happened. He told me to block Mary too, so I did. I did not need this drama in my life now. I was so serious about my future and I wanted to become a physician assistant with Vinnie and that was all I had on my mind. I wanted to make something of myself and I wasn't interested in drugs or drama.

When Vinnie got home I said, "Vinnie, you don't think she overdosed because of me, do you? Because I left her with the apartment after the fight? Her mother made me feel guilty like this was all my fault and she never would have done this if it wasn't for me." Vinnie opened his mouth in shock and narrowed his eyebrows and said, "Absolutely not. THIS IS NOT YOUR FAULT. And I don't want you to ever think it was. That is bullshit and you know it. She was the asshole for taking the drugs and if she wants to kill herself, so be it, but it's NOT your fault Nay. IT'S NOT." I started sobbing. "I didn't even know she was doing drugs, Vinnie, I swear, I didn't know." He hugged me and said, "I know you didn't and neither did I. I had no idea.

Personally, I don't think she was doing drugs and I think her mother lied to you about that. I think she did the drugs after you left to make everyone think it was your fault and for you to feel guilty and it's working. She is pulling the 'poor me' card. I knew she was an asshole when I met her and I was right."

A month went by and Vinnie and I were still working on our classes together and going to our labs at the college. A few times, we both had one on the same night, which was nice. After labs one Friday night, we stopped and got a couple slices of pizza on the way home and brought it home. We had eaten dinner earlier, but we just felt like it, so we had a pizza snack. We sat on the couch to cuddle and relax and watch a little TV. It was about 10:30 p.m. and my phone was ringing. It was a number I didn't recognize, but I picked it up and said, "Hello?" There was a pause and I said, "Hello?" Vinnie grabbed my phone and put it on speaker. He said, "HELLO" in a loud deep voice. I heard a man's voice say, "Renee?" I said, "Yes, this is Renee. Who is this?" He said, "It's Trevor, Rain's dad". I was polite and said, "Oh Hi, how are you?" He said, "I am calling to let you know that Rain died yesterday. She overdosed on drugs 2 days after getting out of Rehab." I just stared into space and the tears came, and I couldn't stop crying. Vinnie took the phone and gave his condolences to Trevor and thanked him for calling.

Trevor told Vinnie he would send the information about the services to my phone once the arrangements were made. He rubbed my back and tried to calm me down. I kept saying, "Oh My God, this is all my fault for moving out on her and yelling at her. It's all my fault." Vinnie held my shoulders in his hands and made me look at him. "THIS IS NOT YOUR FAULT NAY. HOW CAN YOU SAY THAT? SHE WAS NOT A BABY, EVEN THOUGH SHE ACTED LIKE ONE. SHE WAS AN ADULT AND SHE TOOK THE DRUGS ON HER OWN ACCORD. IT'S WHAT SHE WANTED TO DO AND SHE DIDN'T WASTE ANY TIME DOING IT AFTER SHE GOT OUT OF REHAB. THIS HAS NOTHING TO DO WITH YOU NAY. YOU TOOK CARE OF HER WHEN YOU WERE LIVING TOGETHER. YOU DID EVERYTHING YOU COULD FOR HER. END OF STORY. I FEEL BAD THAT SHE DIED AND SHE WAS YOUR FRIEND, BUT IT'S NOT YOUR FAULT AT ALL."

I cried on and off for days, but Vinnie was patient with me the whole time and kept reassuring me that it wasn't my fault. Her father sent me the information on the services in Delaware and Vinnie said he would take me, but if I became too upset, we were leaving.

We drove to Delaware and we both had to take vacation days because she wasn't immediate family. We took our laptops and still did our classes in the hotel. Trevor told us we could stay with them and so did my mom and dad, but we wanted to stay in a hotel. My mom was a little upset, but I explained that we were still doing our classes while we were there, but we would be back and forth. She told us to come there for breakfast, lunch and dinner so we wouldn't have to spend anymore money. We agreed to that. They were both upset over her death as well, and Vinnie didn't want me to keep getting upset. When my mom cried, I cried and it went back and forth.

Vinnie told my mom that, that was the main reason we were in a hotel and she understood. We attended the services and I was happy that it was a closed casket. I cried a little, but I was ok. I went to Mary to tell her I was sorry, but she was very cold to me and pulled away. I didn't want to start anything there, but I would in the future. How dare she blame this on me?

Vinnie told me to let it go. Trevor hugged me and cried and then we left. I didn't want to sit there and be miserable. My parents came with us, paid their respects and we all left together and went out for dinner. Tomorrow was the funeral and we intended on going to it, but not to the celebration of life afterwards. I told Vinnie that I wouldn't be able to be nice to her mom and that would cause trouble, so we skipped it and went back to my mom's house and my dad ordered a couple trays of food.

We checked out of the hotel the next morning and went to say goodbye to my parents and started our drive back to New York. I was over it and pretty much back to normal in a week. I didn't cry over her anymore. Vinnie was right, as usual. It wasn't my fault and I did not feel guilty at all. I didn't give her the drugs and I took care of her when we moved in together and I did everything possible for her. Done deal. It was back to reality for both of us. We got back to work, making dinners and back to our classes. Vinnie was almost done with his classes and I could see he was getting excited about it. I still had 3-4 months left to go and I was getting excited.

9

I thought that I would get through my paramedic job without seeing anything too terrifying, but I didn't. We got called out to a domestic dispute and when we got there, a little boy, maybe 5-6 years old, was on the front lawn, all full of blood and crying his little heart out. The inside of the house was a murder/crime scene. There was blood everywhere, including the walls and ceiling. The father shot his wife and then turned the gun on himself.

Vinnie picked up the little boy and rushed him to the ambulance where he was checked out, to find out where the blood was coming from and it turned out that he was not bleeding at all and that he was probably trying to wake up his mom and it was all her blood. How horrifying this must have been for him! Our team got him cleaned up and removed him from the scene to the hospital and we had to remove the mother and father from the house in body bags, after the police arrived and did their thing because it was a crime scene. I cried more about this call, than I did for Rain, but I cried on my own time (not at the scene). Vinnie said I should do a little therapy for it, but I told him I was fine and I was. It was all part of the job and I did it.

Vinnie finished his Bachelor's degree and was working on his Master's degree from an accredited Physician Assistant program. I was right behind him doing the accredited Physician Assistant program, but I had 3-4 months to go and he was almost finished. We had to sit down and talk about both of our futures, especially after we both graduated. He said he would wait for me to graduate and then we would figure it out, but I wanted him to start looking for a physician's assistant job as soon as he graduated and that he didn't need to wait for me. He insisted. "Maybe we can find a Medical Center that would hire both of us. Actually, I was thinking that before we look for a job, we should take a break. We have saved up vacation time and we should take it, before we leave because if not, we might lose it. I think we should use it all and go somewhere and take a break from work and we will be done with school. We both worked hard for this and we deserve a vacation. A nice vacation. What do you think?" I said, "I think you are right. We have been doing this

for almost 2 years with little vacation time.
Day after day, work and school. Let's do it."

The day finally came when I finished. Vinnie
had already taken the PANCE (Physician
Assistant National Certification Exam) and
passed with flying colors. I was nervous, but I
knew I could do it. It was a 5 hour test that
includes 300 multiple choice questions. I paid
the $550 exam fee and I was studying like
crazy. Vinnie kept asking me if I wanted help
studying, but I refused it. I needed to do this
by myself with no help. I passed the test in the
top of my class and we were both licensed
physician assistants.

My mom and dad gave us both a graduation
party and invited his parents and his brother
and wife, and told them to bring Vinnie's
friends, relatives and whoever else they
wanted and my mom and dad invited all our
relatives and some of my school friends and a
few neighbors. It was a really nice party and
they had a ton of food and it was all set up
outside under a big tent. There were balloons
and flowers and it decorated so nice. They
had a big sheet cake that said,
"CONGRATULATIONS TO RENEE & VINNIE."

I dragged Vinnie around and introduced him to all my friends, relatives and neighbors and I got to meet his parents, a few of his relatives, his brother and his wife and Little Kyle, who was adorable, by the way. He wanted me to hold him, so I carried him around for a while, but he got too heavy, so Vinnie took over. We made about $5,000 at our party, but we banked that money because we had already saved for our vacation.

We stayed at my parents house for a couple of days and his parents wanted us to stay with them for a couple of days.

We were on vacation now and we had planned a trip to Florida so we could sit on the beach and do some site seeing. We went bar hopping, and went to Lion Country Safari in West Palm Beach, we shopped at the Tanger Outlets, we went to Manatee Lagoon and the Palm Beach Zoo. We went on a sunset cruise too, which was very romantic.

One afternoon, we went to the beach and we were walking on the edge of the water, holding hands and talking and he stopped and turned me towards him, kissed me and then got down on one knee and proposed to me. I immediately started tearing up and said, "Yes, Yes. I will marry you." He kissed me and hugged me and he chuckled a little and said,"I couldn't wait to give this to you, because I was afraid I would lose it."

A man came up to us and said, "Congratulations. I know, this is none of my business, but I took a picture of you proposing and I was wondering if you would like to have it." He smiled at Vinnie and me and continued. "I didn't see anyone around taking pictures and thought you would like a momento." Vinnie looked at him and said, "Thank you so much. I never thought about that and I would love it." Vinnie gave him his cell number and he forwarded us the picture and then he showed Vinnie that he was deleting the text. He laughed and said, "I don't want you to think I am a stalker or anything, so I am deleting your number." Vinnie thanked him and he left.

Vinnie took a picture of the ring on my finger and then forwarded that and the picture of him proposing and forwarded it to my family and his. I asked him, "Did anyone know you were doing this?". He smiled and said, "Just my brother. I wanted to do this a long time ago, but I figured it would interrupt our schooling, so I waited." I hugged him and said, "I am glad you waited."

So now both of our phones were blowing up with Congrats texts and he just smiled at me. "I love you so much Nay. I promise I will make you happy and protect you, in every way possible, forever." I said, "I love _you_ more, Vinnie and I will make you happy forever."

Our vacation went by fast and we flew back to New York and settled in. We went back to work 4 days later and Vinnie told his boss that we both graduated and we were looking for a job. That's just the way he was. He wanted his boss to know ahead of time, so he had plenty of time to replace us. That's not to say we even looked yet or that we would both get a job at the same time, but he wanted to let him know and his boss shook his hand and told him that he appreciated the heads up.

We looked for jobs in Medical Centers first and there was nothing available. I told Vinnie we should look at hospitals because we had a better chance there. There were tons and I mean tons of job openings for physician's assistants and a lot of them were in the Emergency Department. He looked at me and said, "Should we apply? All of a sudden, I am scared of leaving my job. Like, what if I don't like it, what if they don't like me, what if…" I interrupted him. "Uh oh, cold feet? Vinnie, you are so smart and you know exactly what you are doing, so don't second guess yourself and stop with the What if's. We are gonna do this. We both worked hard for almost 2 years to get this, so let's do it. We are applying today." He smiled at me and said, "See, this is why *you caught my eye*. You always make me come back to my senses and I need you."

We applied for the jobs at the Mt. Sinai Hospital. This is the same hospital where I arrived after being punched in the head. Both jobs were in the Emergency Department. We were both called for Interviews and we were both hired. We called our parents to let them know and everyone was excited for us. We were starting in 2 weeks and Vinnie called his boss to let him know. He congratulated both of us and said that he had 2 people lined up for our jobs. That made Vinnie nervous and I reminded him how long it took us to get where we are.

In the meantime, both sets of parents were setting up our wedding and texting us asking us what we wanted and where we wanted it and so forth. My parents were paying for the wedding and his parents insisted on paying for their guests and the rehearsal dinner, the night before. I was so happy that our parents got along. My mom and his mom became best friends. My parents drove to New York and stayed with them for a weekend and my dad and his dad and brother were best buddies.

We were laying in bed and relaxing and I was thinking that my whole life seemed like a dream come true. I had an awesome guy that really and truly cared for me. Our parents got along, we finished our schooling and became physician's assistants and got a job at the local hospital.   What more could we ask for?

I dozed off. My phone was ringing and I answered it. "Is this Ms. Renee Madden?" I answered and looked at the clock. It was 3:10 a.m. "Yes, it is. Who is this?" I heard the voice on the other end of the phone. "This is

Mt. Sinai Hospital and I am sorry to inform you that Vincent Greco has passed away after the accident." I froze. "What are you talking about?. NOOO. NOOO. I was crying and started screaming. NOOO, THIS CAN'T BE. HE IS RIGHT HERE WITH ME". I looked over and he was gone. I was screaming at the top of my lungs. NOOO. VINNIE!!! WHERE ARE YOU VINNIE? OMG VINNIE WHERE ARE YOU?"

I woke up in a sweat. I was soaked in sweat and it was dripping down my face and Vinnie was right there, holding me tight and dabbing my face with a tissue. "I am right here babe. I am right here. You were having a nightmare. I was still screaming. "OMG. VINNIE WHERE ARE YOU". I heard him. "NAY WAKE UP YOU ARE HAVING A NIGHTMARE" He was tapping me in the face with his fingers. I was awake. I looked at him and said, "They called me from the hospital and told me you were in an accident and they said you died. Oh My GOD Vinnie. This is bad." He hugged me tight and assured me he was not in an accident and he was very much alive. "It's ok Babe". He was rocking me in his arms. "I am ok. I am alive and it was just a dream." I said, "They even said your name 'Vincent Greco'. I heard them." He assured me it was a dream and he continued rocking me in his arms while I sobbed for over an hour. I could have sworn that it was real. I will never, ever forget that nightmare, for as long as I live. It was the worst nightmare I ever had in my life and now I was paranoid that something was going to happen to him and that the nightmare was a warning.

I didn't sleep for the rest of the night and neither did Vinnie. He held me till morning and kept assuring me that he was ok. I just stared at the ceiling and the tears kept streaming down my face. I couldn't help it, because it seemed so real. I can still hear that voice and if I hear it again, I would recognize it. Please GOD, do not let me hear that voice again.

It was 8:30 a.m. and I must have dozed off again, but I was still scared when I woke up. I was afraid to fall asleep again, but I was so tired and groggy from being up all night. I looked over and Vinnie was sleeping. I didn't want to wake him, so I just laid there and I must have dozed off again. I heard him stirring in the bed and he got up to use the bathroom and came right back.

He got in bed and got right up against me and put his arm around me. "You awake babe?" I moaned a little so he knew I heard him. He said, "You are ok, and so am I. It was just a nightmare and I know that it seemed real, but sometimes nightmares are like that. I don't want you to keep worrying about it ok?" I opened my eyes and he was right over my head looking at me.

"I love you Vinnie and I would die without you. I mean it. I can't live without you. You are my soul mate, so you can't die on me." He smiled and said, "I am not going anywhere and I love you more."

10

All I can say is that I was happy it was a Saturday. I was walking around in a cloud and couldn't think straight and I am not sure if it was because of the nightmare or the fact that I only slept about 3 hours. Vinnie whipped up some pancakes and sausages and I made some coffee and set the table. I felt bad for keeping him awake all night. I came up behind him at the stove and hugged him around the chest. "Sorry I kept you awake all night." He turned around and hugged me. "You don't have to apologize. That was one hell of a nightmare hon. I felt so bad for you." He turned around and flipped the pancakes. "Pancakes coming up in 30 seconds."

He served them and I got the sausages to the table. He sat down and said, "Are you ok?" I told him I was, but scared something was gonna happen and wondered why I had that dream. I told him that if I ever heard that voice again, I would flip out. He tilted his head and looked at me and said, "I know it's hard, but try to forget about it. Wanna take a ride to my brother's house today?" I said, "Yeah, that would be nice, but you should let him know we are coming." He texted his brother and they were happy we were coming. His brother called him on the phone because he hates texting. His brother told us to plan on staying for dinner. We finished breakfast and I told Vinnie I would clean up, because he was still talking to his brother. He went out on the deck to talk to him, so I am sure he told him what happened.

I went in to take a shower and get all the dried sweat off of me. I got dressed and then changed the sheets on the bed because they were all wet from my sweating. They were dry now, but still, I didn't want to sleep in them tonight. Vinnie came in as I was putting the clean sheets on and helped me with the other side to make it quicker. He was such a good guy. There aren't too many guys out there that would do that, but I guess because he did it when he was alone, I was actually helping him. LOL. He helped me with the pillow cases and the comforter and we were done in no time.

He went in to take a shower and got dressed and we took off for his brother's, about an hour later. He kept looking at me and checking on me and I know he was still worried about me. Hell, I was worried about me. It was gonna take awhile to stop thinking about this. This was the first time going to his brother's house and he was about 10 miles north of his parents house, so he was pointing things out to me.

It was an hour away from Vinnie's house, going north, but it was a comfortable ride, after we got out of the city. His brother's house had more of a country setting and we even went by a farm and saw cows and horses. We stopped at a roadside market to see what they had for sale and Vinnie picked up some zucchini, a head of lettuce, a dozen corn on the cob, some tomatoes and a cucumber. He told me he always brought something when he was invited for dinner. He hasn't been to his brother's house in a couple of years because of school and work, so he was excited. He saw him, when he visited his parents, of course, but hasn't been to the house.

His brother had a beautiful house with 4 bedrooms and 2 1/2 baths. He had a dining room, living room, a huge deck, and an above ground pool with a big backyard. His deck had tiki lights all around and they had a big tent on it with music playing. They had a barbecue and gate at the top of the stairs so the baby wouldn't fall down the stairs. They had a bunch of toys out there for him.

I felt so comfortable here. They made it very welcoming and they treated me like one of the family. The guys made margaritas and I sat outside with Maria and Kyle and Vinnie and Jimmie were inside gabbing and drinking a beer. Maria was so sociable and kept the conversation going. She asked about the classes we took and the test and how me and Vinnie were making out, living together. We never had a quiet moment and we got along very well. It was really the first time we were alone and really got to know each other.

The weather was perfect. It was the beginning of September, so it wasn't hot and wasn't cold. They had the pool covered already for the winter months. Vinnie and Jimmie came out and they watched Kyle while Maria showed me around the yard. It was a really big backyard and they had a lot of beautiful flowers and pretty bushes. She pointed things out to me and we walked around the yard to the front and then around to the back again. She said, "I hope this wasn't too boring. I needed a break from Kyle." She started laughing and then said, "Even if it's for 10 minutes. He is such a handful. Thankfully Jimmie is big help." I laughed and said, "I actually enjoyed the walk and seeing your pretty flowers, so anytime you want to show me again, go for it." She looked at me and said, "I love the fuck out of you Nay." She paused for a minute as we walked up the stairs to the deck and then said, "Jimmie is gonna make a couple of pork tenderloins on the grill. I hope you like pork and if you don't, I can take something else out for you to eat." I told her that I loved pork tenderloin. She said, "Oh, excellent. I made some salad sides and Vinnie brought the corn on the cob, so we are having that too." I patted her on the shoulder. "I am not fussy, unless you feed me liver. I draw the line there." She looked at me and opened her mouth and put her finger in it and made a vomit sound. "KEH KEH, UGH." We walked up the stairs and she opened the gate and we sat back in our lawn chairs. Jimmie asked me if I wanted another Margarita and I said, "Yes, please. It was really good." Maria said, "I will join her." Kyle was running around the deck and playing with his toys. Vinnie said, "I'll be right back. I forgot, I got him a gift and it's in the trunk."

He came back with a big brown paper bag and sat on the deck floor with the bag and Kyle ran up to him and he was trying to peek in the bag and Vinnie was teasing him and then he let him peek into a corner of the bag and then he told him to sit down and would give him the bag. Kyle sat and Vinnie handed him the bag. He had the biggest smile on his face and Vinnie took a picture as he pulled out a big Ambulance that had a siren and he showed him how to use it.

Jimmie looked at his brother and said, "You are taking that home bro, cause I am not listening to that all day." Vinnie just laughed at him. "Let him play with it for a while and then just take the batteries out and tell him it's broken. Jimmie laughed and said, "If you buy him drums for Christmas, I am disowning you." We all laughed.

I really needed this to bring me out of my funk. By the end of the day, I was feeling so much better. Tired, but better. We had a nice dinner and I helped Maria clean up. She told me she likes to clean up because it gives her a break from Kyle and Jimmie gets to spend some time with him. She laughed and said, "Work slower." I laughed with her and she was giggling. "You must think I am a bad mother, but wait till you have a child and you will know what I am talking about." I looked at her and said, "I do not think that at all and I think you are hysterical."

We said our goodbyes and we promised that we would have them over for dinner, once we got settled with our new jobs.

We had a nice ride home and it was still a little light out, so I got to see some pretty leaves on the way. It took us a little over an hour because of some traffic, but we weren't in any hurry. Vinnie had a smile on his face and I knew he had a good time with his brother and that he missed him. I looked at him and said, "It was such a nice day. I like it up there. We should do this more often." He smiled at me and said, "We will. We will do this more often."

We got into our PJ's and slumped into the couch to watch some TV and then headed to bed after the news. I told Vinnie I was afraid to fall asleep and he told me to try to forget about. "Just let yourself fall asleep and you will, because you are exhausted." Of course, he was right. My head hit the pillow and I was out like a light. I slept all night with no dreams or nightmares, at least none that I could remember. I was relieved when I woke up the next morning. I smelled coffee, and that is because it was right under my nose. I opened my eyes and Vinnie was looking down at me with a cup in his hand. He put it on the night table and then he got in bed next to me with his cup. We sat in bed and sipped coffee and he asked me if I slept good without dreams and I told him I did. He said, "I don't even remember falling asleep and I slept all night without waking up."

We sat there sipping coffee and talking for about a half hour and then we got up to shower and dress. I said, "What are we doing today? Any plans?" He said, "Well I thought we could go to the Country Fair. It opens today. It's got a carnival atmosphere, but they have animals, contests, food, horse races and games. I think you would like it. Wanna go?" My face lit up and I said, "Yeah, that sounds awesome."

We left the house around 11:00 and went to the fair. I loved fairs and I was so excited to get there. It was everything I expected and more and we had such a good time. We spent the whole day there and we ate and drank and played games and saw everything they had. We sat on a bench to rest because we had walked miles.

A woman came up to Vinnie and said, "Hey handsome, wanna roll in the hay?" He looked up at her and said, "What the fuck did you just say?" She was practically in his lap and he was shooing her away and she said, "I don't stutter, what do you say?" He stood up and got in her face and said, "Get the fuck out of here NOW." She backed up and said, "You don't have to be mean, just say no." He said, "GET THE FUCK OUT OF HERE AND LEAVE ME ALONE."

I was just sitting there unable to understand what the fuck just happened. This happens at a fair? Usually it's a bar, but I never thought something like this would happen at a fair. I told him to check his wallet. "Did she get close enough to you that she could take something out of your jacket?" He checked and nothing was taken. He said, "Well, that just ruined my day. Wanna go before anything else happens?" I looked at him and said, "We have seen everything we needed to see, we ate and we had fun. Don't let her ruin your day. Let's go."

We started walking to the car and Vinnie looked in the distance at his car and she was standing near it with a big guy. He stopped walking and said, "Let's find a cop because I think there is going to be trouble.

How the hell do they know that's my car?" I looked and saw her and the guy near our car. He saw a cop and started walking towards him. I was keeping an eye on the girl and when they saw us going for the cop, they walked away from the car.

Vinnie told the cop what happened and that they were near his car. The cop offered to walk us to our car and Vinnie let him. He thanked him and we got in and locked the doors and the cop stayed there until we left the parking lot. I knew Vinnie was scared and I didn't want to say anything right away. I was going to let him start the conversation. He didn't say anything until we got on the highway. "I wonder what they wanted? Were they gonna roll me? Take all our stuff? Kill us? I don't know anyone that hates me so what the fuck?" I kept quiet because I was scared too. He looked at me and said, "You ok?" I shook my head yes. I was thinking that we should move more upstate where his parents and brother were in the country, but we just got jobs down here. I wonder if we could transfer upstate? I didn't think this was the right time to say anything or not, so I will wait till we get home. It was pretty quiet on the ride home and I knew he was really upset because he is never quiet.

11

We pulled into the driveway and there was a box on our porch. It was a medium size box and it was addressed to me. It wasn't from Amazon or any store and no return address. Vinnie picked it up and brought it inside. He shook it and then said, "You want me to open it?" I shook my head yes. I had no idea who it could be from. I noticed initials in the return address area that said MP, but that was all there was. Vinnie opened the box and I looked inside. There was a note on top. It was from Mary Parker, Rain's mom.

Dear Renee:

I am sending you these things that belonged to Rain. She wanted you to have them. Apparently, her death was a suicide. She planned all of it and she marked everything in her room that she was leaving to everyone. You will see her note in the bottom of the box. I am sorry that I blamed this on you. I know you will never forgive me for it, but I am sorry.

Love Mary

Vinnie and I looked at each other and tears came immediately to my eyes. She had been my friend since Kindergarten and I still had feelings for her, even after what she did to me and how she acted. In the box was a card that I gave her for her 16th birthday and I had written a long note to her and tucked it inside on how much she meant to me and what a good friend she was. I remembered writing that note like it was yesterday and I cried while reading it.

I picked up a small box and inside was a red stuffed cardinal bird that I gave her. It was her favorite bird. She put a post-it note on it and it said, "When you see a cardinal in your window, it will be me, visiting you." I broke down crying after seeing that, and I had to wait to see what else was in the box after I settled down. The guilt trip was on me and I felt so bad for yelling at her and treating her like I did. I must have hurt her to the point of suicide. Vinnie kept telling me that I was NOT the reason that she committed suicide. He calmed me down. I continued to look in the box and there was a little jewelry box and when I opened it, I completely lost it. It was the other half of my heart that I wore around my neck. She bought it and gave one half to me. Vinnie grabbed the box and took it away from me. "That is enough for today. This is too much for anyone to handle, even me."

He calmed me down, like he always did. He cuddled with me and we rolled around on the bed and had some great sex. We laid there for a long time and then he ordered take out from the Fish Fry down the street.

12

"Vinnie? I have been thinking and I have an idea, but you probably don't wanna do it." He laughed and said, "What makes you say that? I usually am up for anything you suggest." I said, "Well, this is pretty big, so…." He put his arm around me and said, "Tell me". I said, "Well, I know we just got jobs at the hospital, but I was wondering if you would be willing to move up towards your brothers house and maybe we could transfer our jobs up to the Mt Sinai near him?" He pulled away to look at me and said, "Really? You want to move up there? It gets really cold and snowy up there. I mean, that wouldn't bother me, but it's really cold in the winter." I told him I didn't care about the weather. "We can always go to Florida for a few weeks in the winter." He smiled at me and said, "If that is what you want, we will do it. Even if we can't transfer our jobs, we can get new ones. I would love to live near my brother." I had a surprised look on my face and all of a sudden I was so excited. "Really

Vinnie? Really?" He smiled at me lovingly and said, "Anything for you. You know that. It's for me too." He started laughing.

Later that evening, we went online to look for jobs at the Mt. Sinai near his brother and they had tons of openings, so we would just wait till we were ready to move. We started to pack up stuff we weren't using and we piled boxes in the garage all labeled and sealed.

We had his brother looking for houses up near him and he would send them to Vinnie. Jimmie and Maria were so excited that we were going to live up that way, not to mention his parents. My parents on the other hand, were a little upset that we were moving an hour more north, away from them, but they said they would still visit.

We started cleaning up the house and hitting the inside with paint to touch up some areas and make it look sellable. We had a cracked tile in the bathroom, but Vinnie hired a guy to fix that. Otherwise, the house was in great shape and he hired a real estate agent to sell it. Jimmie and Maria told us that if we needed a place to stay until we closed, we could stay with them.

In the meantime, we started our jobs at the hospital and it was crazy, crazy in that emergency room. I never saw so much commotion and drama in one place. I wasn't sure I liked it and told Vinnie that I thought it was a little too much for me. He admitted that he didn't like it either and that we should look for a medical center or a doctor's office when we moved.

We had saved a lot of money together, so we would be good for a while without a job, if we needed to rely on that. Jimmie told us not to worry about it because we could stay with them. He sent us quite a few houses for sale and one of them was down the street from him and when he sent it to Vinnie, he had circled it and starred it in red marker. Vinnie chuckled when he saw it and he showed me. It was just like his brother's house and it wasn't overly expensive. Vinnie said if we couldn't find a physician assistant jobs, we could still be paramedics. "We have that under our belt, so we will be ok and we will make enough money to afford it." He paid $175,000 for the house he had now and the real estate agent told him he could easily get $225,000 for it now and he would push for it. He had quite a bit of equity in the house, so we would use that as a down payment on the new house. We were all set, so all we had to do was sell this house and buy a new one.

Vinnie's house went on the market and the first weekend, there was an open house, so we took a ride to his brother's for the whole weekend and booked an appointment to see the house down the street from him. Jimmie and Maria (and little Kyle) went with us. We all loved it, so we put in an offer on Saturday and it was accepted on Sunday. We were so excited. Vinnie picked me up and he was swinging me around and Jimmy and Maria were laughing and they were excited for us too. Vinnie said, "Now we just have to sell the other one. I hope the open house went good."

We drove home that night and got our stuff ready for work the next day. The house was still neat and clean but we noticed some foot prints, so Vinnie wiped them up with a wet sponge. We prepped one meal for the next day because that is all we had time for.

The next day, we went to work and Vinnie got a phone call from the real estate agent and told him that there was a bidding war going on with 4 people that wanted the house. He told Vinnie that everyone loved the house. Vinnie was surprised and texted me right away.

Although we were both in the same Emergency Department, on the same floor, we rarely saw each other, because it was so crazy and it was a big department. I read his text and couldn't believe it. He told me he texted his brother already. He said the top bidder, so far, was $245,000. I couldn't wait to leave now and I was so excited. I wanted to quit this job today. I hated it, I mean I <u>really</u> hated it.

Vinnie and I clocked out and went home and we talked about the move all the way home. We stopped at Home Depot on the way home for some more boxes and packing tape and bubble wrap. He said, "I think we should pack up the kitchen stuff tonight, after we eat, and live off of paper dishes and plastic forks and eat out. We need to pack up the living room entertainment center, except for the big stuff and the TV." I was bubbling over with happiness and excitement. I could tell Vinnie was too. He was babbling off, what we should pack and what we should buy and when we should do certain things. I just looked at him and I could see in his eyes and smile how happy he was. I said, "How long do you think it will take before the closing on this house and the new one?" He said, "Hmm. Maybe a week or so. What are you thinking?" I laughed and said, "I am thinking when I can quit that fucking job and stay home." He busted out laughing and said, "Yeah, me too. Is tomorrow enough time?" I said through my giggling. "Yup, sounds good to me. Let's give our notice and make it one week instead of two." I paused and said, "I would rather stay home and pack than to have to go back there." He put his hand on my shoulder. "Tomorrow it is. Let's do it."

We left Home Depot and went home.   I put the casserole in the oven and we sat down to eat and we ate in paper dishes, so there wouldn't be any dirty dishes. The dishwasher had nothing in it and we wanted to keep it that way. We cleaned up dinner and got to work and packed up the whole kitchen. Everything was empty.

I helped Vinnie take the boxes to the garage and he stacked everything up. We were parking in the driveway now so we would have room for all the boxes. We started on the living room and packed everything up except the big stuff and took those boxes out to the garage. The bathroom stuff was last, so we went into the closet and just brought out boxes that were already packed from when I moved in. All that was left was the bathroom, our clothes and the furniture. Vinnie got $250,000 for the house and the closings were back to back, which was nice. First the closing on the old house and then the new one, which worked out perfectly.

We gave our notice and the ER was shocked, but we explained that we were unexpectedly moving an hour north. We had 4 days of work left and it couldn't come fast enough. We actually only worked 2 of those days and took our only 2 vacations days that we had coming. We hired a moving company and they packed up the whole house on Thursday. The closing on the old house was Thursday night and the closing on the new house was Friday afternoon. We told the moving company to deliver on Friday after 2:00 p.m. We had to pay extra for that, but I guess they get that all the time.

We were completely out on Thursday night and we drove up to his brother's house, after the closing, that night with an overnight bag and everyone was so excited. I followed Vinnie with my car and he was nervous about that, but we did fine. We spent one night at his brothers house and went to the closing on the new house the next day and our moving truck was waiting outside when we got there.

Jimmie and Maria came to help us move in and Maria's parents were babysitting for Kyle. A car pulled up outside when we were unlocking our new house. It was Vinnie's parents and his mother was sobbing and happy that we moved closer. They came to help us and Vinnie was super happy about that. Jimmie told us to get our bedroom and bathroom situated first and the rest could wait. Jimmy and Vinnie put the bed together and me and Maria made it up with the sheets and comforter. Rosa put the bathroom together for us and his father, Jay, was helping Jimmy and Vinnie, in the living room with the TV, the Playstation and stereo equipment.

We had boxes everywhere. Some were open and some were still sealed, but everything was labeled so we knew what was in them. Maria and I put clothes in the closet and Rosa started in the kitchen with the silverware and then came in to ask where we wanted dishes and pots and pans so I went in to show her and Maria stayed in the closet doing clothes. The movers put the patio table and chairs on the deck for us, along with the barbecue and extra tables.

We were fully moved in by Sunday afternoon and all the boxes were flattened and stacked in the garage. Jimmy and Maria had everyone over for dinner, Friday and Saturday night and me and Vinnie took everyone out for dinner on Sunday afternoon to a really nice restaurant.

I absolutely loved my new house and so did Vinnie, but the best part for him, was that he was close to his brother. My parents apologized for not coming to help, but I told them that I did not expect them to drive so far for that and I would rather they came to visit for a long weekend, rather than have them moving boxes.

13

Vinnie and I were settled in and looking for jobs. We went on a couple of interviews and then we saw an ad for 2 physician assistants for a husband and wife, that had a practice together, right here in town, near our house. We didn't waste any time and applied for the positions and got interviews. We didn't hide the fact that we were engaged to each other and they were actually happy about that. The wife wanted me to be her assistant and the husband wanted Vinnie to be his assistant.

They showed us around the building and introduced us to everyone. They had a blood drawing station there and they did ultrasounds and x-rays, right in the same building. The place was awesome and I knew it was the right place for us. I knew it in my heart that this was our destination. We were home. On our way home, Vinnie said, "This was meant to be Nay. It was meant to be." I smiled at him and said, "I agree 100% and I was just saying that to myself, that in my heart, I knew it was our destination and we were home." We got home in 5 minutes and I had made some taco meat and Spanish rice, before we left, so we made some tacos and had supper in our new dining room.

We bought a brand new dining room set, when we moved in, because we didn't have a dining room in Vinnie's old house. We knew it was probably going to be the last one we ever bought, so we bought a really good set and it was friggin beautiful.

We finished supper and I was cleaning up and my phone was ringing. It was Trevor. I looked at Vinnie and he said, "What the hell does he want now?" I answered, "Hi Trevor, How are you?" He said, "I just wanted you to know that Mary had a heart attack and she is in Saint Francis Hospital. She will be ok. I guess I just needed someone to talk to." He pulled at my heart strings. "Oh Trevor, I am so so sorry. Did she have a blockage?" He said, "Yes, and they put stents in her artery." I assured him that she would be fine and he said, "Rain broke her heart Nay and she will never be the same. All she does is cry and she is depressed and she won't go anywhere or do anything." I told him that she needs to see a doctor for the depression and told him not to wait. He said, "I know, but how do I get her there?" I said, "Trevor? She is at the hospital right now. It's the perfect place. Talk to the doctor and tell him/her what's going on and they will take it from there. Promise me you will do that ok?" He said he would. I said, "Are you ok Trevor? Do you need anything?" He said he was fine and it was good to hear my voice. I told him that we moved to Upstate New York and bought a new house and he congratulated us. He said, "I miss her Nay. I miss her so bad. I'm sorry, I shouldn't be laying this on you." I said, "It's ok Trevor. Everything will be ok and if you are depressed, then you need to see a doctor too." He said, he would see a doctor and then hung up.

I put my phone on the table and Vinnie looked at me. "He is lonely Nay. It is hard to lose a child and then have his wife have a heart attack. He is probably scared to death. I think you helped him a little and you were there for him. That's all that counts. It sounds like you were their second daughter." I said, "I was. I was always there at their house and that is why they always call me." Vinnie said, "Call him back and ask if you can visit. You can go see Mary in the hospital and visit him and your parents. Let's do it before we start our new jobs." I did not hesitate. I called Trevor back. He answered right away. "Hi Nay, HI." I said, "Trevor, would it be ok if we came to visit you? We want to see Mary in the hospital too and I can visit my parents while I am there. Vinnie and I just got new jobs and we start in 2 weeks, so it would just be a quick visit." I heard the excitement in his voice. "YES, Yes, I would love it if you came to visit. I would love it. When are you coming?" I had him on speaker phone and Vinnie said, "Tomorrow?" He was so happy. "Tomorrow? Really? Yes, yes. Oh honey, I miss seeing you." I said, "I know Trevor, I miss seeing you too. We will see you tomorrow around noon?" He said, "I will be waiting. Mary will be so happy to see you too." We hung up and I called my parents and told them we were coming and what happened with Mary. They were happy that we were visiting and said to pick them up before we went to Trevor's and the hospital and they would go with us. We talked for a bit and then hung up.

I went to hug Vinnie and said, "Thanks Babe. I appreciate this so much." He pulled me down into his lap and pulled me close and said, "I said it before and I will say it again. I will do anything for you, because I love the fuck out of you."

The next morning, we got up early, showered and dressed and started our trip to Delaware. We stopped at a diner to get some breakfast and we were on our way. When we got there, we went to my parents house and we were talking about what Vinnie had said about me being their second daughter and that they needed me now. My mom agreed and said, "Well, you were always at their house and for them it was like having 2 kids and it was the same for me, because I always felt like Rain was my second daughter." I told her how Mary sent me a box, but the stuff she sent me was making me cry, so Vinnie took it away. I told her what I saw so far, and she started to cry. She said, "I remember buying that little stuffed cardinal at the card store for you to give to her. That was soooo long ago." We were at their house for about 1/2 hour. We left at 7:30 am., stopped for breakfast and it took a little more than 4 hours to get there and it was 12:30. Vinnie said we should get going and so we all piled in the car. I sat in the back with my mom and my dad sat up front with Vinnie.

Trevor was only a couple miles up the road. He was smiling from ear to ear when we pulled up into the driveway. We all got out of the car and he started crying. He grabbed me and hugged me so tight. "Thank you for this honey. I can't tell you what this means to me." He shook hands with Vinnie and my dad and hugged my mom. We went inside and he had a nice lunch waiting for us. I know he ordered it from somewhere because Trevor was not a cook, at all. Mary always did the cooking when I was at their house.

We all ate lunch and then headed to the hospital to see Mary. Trevor squished in the backseat with me and mom. The look on Mary's face when we all walked into the room was priceless. She couldn't believe I was there with everyone. She put her arms out to me and I leaned over her and she kept saying. "I am so sorry. I never meant to hurt you in any way. I am sorry I blamed you. I'm sorry honey." I told her not to worry about it. I told her it was over and in the past and that she was forgiven. Trevor leaned over to kiss her and so did my mom and dad and we were all talking and laughing.

I said, "I am thirsty. I am going to get something to drink. Trevor, come with me ok?" He agreed. I got him outside the room and said, "This is your chance. Let's find a nurse and see if we can leave a message for her doctor about the depression." He smiled at me and said, "Ha, Thirsty? Ha ha." He held my arm and we walked to the nurses station where he told her nurse about the depression and how bad it was and why this was happening.

The nurse shook her head and said, "Ok Mr. Parker. I will leave a message for her doctor. It's a good thing you brought this to our attention." He smiled and thanked her and we went to get something to drink. On the way to get some sodas, I told him that he did the right thing and he hugged me. We got a bunch of soda's from the machine and we brought them back to the room. Vinnie smiled at me because he knew what I just did.

We stayed at the hospital for 2 hours and then headed back to Trevor's house. He was so thankful that we made the trip. We told him that we had to start heading back because it was a 4 hour drive. We left and dropped off my parents and headed back to New York. We got home around 8:15 p.m. It was a long day and we were tired and hungry. We didn't stop to eat anything. Vinnie wanted to order food, but I told him we had leftover Taco meat and we should finish it out. He smiled and said, "No arguments out of me." We had a couple of tacos and some Spanish Rice and then cleaned up.

I was so tired and plopped on the couch while Vinnie went in to take a shower. I woke up in bed and I was in my PJ's. How the fuck did that happen? Vinnie was smiling at me, when I turned to find him. "What happened?" It was 11:00 p.m. He said, "You were out like a light. I carried you to the bed and you didn't even move, so I got you in your nightgown, which wasn't easy and here you are." I looked at him with my mouth open and said, "Really, I didn't even move?" He said, "You must have been really tired, because you were dead weight." I laughed and said, "Thanks." He said, "Want some Ice Cream?" I smiled at him and said, "UMM. Yeah." We both got up and went to the kitchen and he scooped out some ice cream into a couple bowls and we sat on the couch and ate it while watching the news. He took the bowls and put them in the sink and rinsed them out. He came back to the couch and started kissing me and he was all over me hugging and kissing me everywhere. He turned off the TV and carried me back to the bed, where he continued and we made love.

14

We still had a week and a half before we started our new jobs, but we got a call from the doctors offices to come in and get our jackets and uniforms. We drove down the street to the office and picked them up and we tried them on. They were just jackets with our names embroidered on them. I had them put Renee Greco on my jacket, because we were getting married in a couple weeks. We were allowed to wear whatever pants we wanted, except no jeans were allowed, and a nice top. We both put a jacket on and they took our pictures, separately and then together.

We thought it was for a badge or something, but we were actually being featured in the Town Newspaper (The Hudson Press) as the new Physician Assistants for Crowley and Crowley, M.D. We didn't know this, until they sent us a copy by email. Vinnie came running out of his office. "NAY, NAY, LOOK AT THIS FUCKING SHIT." I ran to him and he had printed it out. I freaked out. "OMG. HOLY SHIT. THIS IS FUCKING AWESOME." We were shitting our pants, we were so proud of our accomplishment. He sent it to his brother and parents and I sent it to my parents and Trevor and Mary. We both hugged and danced around the living room. Vinnie said, "This is BIG Nay. This is BIG stuff." I was so emotional over this and so was Vinnie. He had tears in his eyes, but he quickly wiped them with his fingers, but I just cried happy tears. He said, "Do you know how proud this makes me?" I smiled lovingly at him and said, "Yes I do hon, yes I do, because I feel the same way. We worked really hard for this and we deserve it."

So our wedding day was coming up as well as our first day on our new job. I still had to go get my wedding gown and Vinnie had to get a tux. He went with his brother, Gary, (his friend) and his Dad. Vinnie drove me, his mom and Maria down to Delaware so we could get our gowns and dresses with my mom and Mary.

We got everything done in one weekend. The men went on a Friday night to get the tuxes and we needed the whole weekend because of travel time. Trevor and my Dad got their tuxes when we got there. The ladies picked a light cranberry color, which I loved and my mom made sure that the same color was in the flowers.

Our wedding was the weekend after our first week of work and we were a little stressed over that. Vinnie said, "What do you think would happen if we asked the doctors if we could have an extra week before we started?" That way we could get married and go on a honeymoon for a week and then come back and start work." I looked at him and said, "All they can say is no. Let's ask, but I think we should ask in person."

He called the office and asked to speak with one of the doctors. They were both busy, but the receptionist said she would leave a message for both of them. An hour later, Mr. Dr. Crowley called back and sounded nervous. Vinnie had him on speaker phone. "Hi, Dr. Crowley. I was wondering if Renee and I could come down to talk to you quickly? I know you are super busy." He said, "Sure, Is there a problem?" Vinnie told him there was something he wanted to run by him, so he told us to come right down because they were both in between patients. We got in the car and went down. They both took us in the office and they looked worried. Vinnie was smiling and said, "There is nothing wrong but we wanted to ask you if it would be possible to start one week later, because we are getting married the weekend after our original start date, so if its ok, we wanted to know if starting a week later would be a problem? We want to go on a honeymoon for a week and when we get back we are 100% yours."

They both sighed and Ms. Dr. Crowley said, "OMG, you both scared us." Mr. Dr. Crowley said, "That is not a problem at all. I would rather see you do that, then start and then leave for a week. You could have told us on the phone." Vinnie smiled at him and said, "That would have been rude. We wanted to ask you in person. If it is a problem, we can just get married and put our honeymoon off for a while." Mr. Crowley shook his head no. "No, No. We want you both to be happy. Go get married and go on your honeymoon and then you can both start and I thank you both for coming to talk to us in person. We thought we were going to lose you both before you started."

Vinnie and I laughed and he said, "We would never do that to you. We applied for the job, knowing that our wedding was coming up, but we didn't want to lose the opportunity to get this job. We just moved here from the City." Mr. Crowley patted him on the back and said, "See you both in a few weeks and Congrats on your marriage. Where are you going for your honeymoon?" Vinnie whispered in his ear. He said, "Ah yes, Great place." We left and we were happy and so were the doctors.

We got in the car and I said, "Vinnie, where <u>are</u> we going on our honeymoon? I didn't even know we had something planned." He looked at me and smiled. "It's a surprise."

We got home and I had a message on my phone. I had it on silent while we were talking to the doctors. It was from Attorney Castillo. I said to Vinnie. "I forgot all about him. We haven't heard from him since my deposition almost 2 years ago." He said, "The courts are backed up, so it takes a long time to settle these cases." I knew the case was coming up for trial or maybe it already did, but we never heard from him. The message said, "I was able to settle your case before going to trial. Give me a call and I will let you know the settlement figure. You will have to approve it, of course, but call me and I will run it by you, before I tell Defendant's counsel it's final."

I called him right back and he said, "How does $40,000 sound?" I almost had a heart attack and I paused. "Umm. Yes, Yes. I am in shock. You got that much?" He laughed and said, "I guess that's a yes?" Vinnie was looking at me with wide eyes and wanted to know how much. I whispered to him. *"$40,000"*. Now he looked like he was going to have a heart attack. I said, "Yes, It's a yes. Absolutely yes."   He said, "Ok, then it's a done deal, like I thought it would be. You should receive your check in a couple weeks. Let's make sure we have your address correct?" I said, "Oh, we moved. We are in Upstate New York now." I gave him our new address and we hung up.

Vinnie and I were jumping up and down holding each other. "OMG VINNIE OMG. THIS IS FUCKING AWESOME." He still couldn't believe it. I couldn't believe it. "The lawyer takes a third right, so we should get around $26,000?" Vinnie said, "He may not take that much. I know for my case, he only took 5,000 and I got quite a bit too. That is how I got a down payment for my house. I bet he takes about $10,000. He is a good guy. You will probably get around $30,000. This is fantastic."

It was wedding time and my parents and Rain's parents took a train instead of driving 4 hours and they all stayed with us.

We all went to really nice restaurant after our rehearsal at the church. Vinnie's parents and brother paid for everything. The next morning was our wedding at 11:00 a.m. The ceremony was elegant and gorgeous and Vinnie wrote me a poem after we said our vows. I will never, ever forget it and I cry when I think about it.

You caught my eye;

You caught my heart;

I'm Flying high;

With that little Spark;

You blew me away;

With your beautiful eyes;

Now I know I'll stay;

Because you are my prize.

It gets me, every time I hear it. He was the most romantic guy I ever met. I loved him so much and the only reason I met him was because I got punched in a bar and he was MY paramedic. Now I was his wife and I was so happy.

My parents gave us the most beautiful reception with all the relatives and friends and everyone had a really good time. There was a lot of dancing and talking and laughing. We got some really nice gifts and a LOT of money.

We had our suitcases packed and I kept asking him where we were going and he said, "Pack your bathing suits." I said, "VINNIE. YOU HAVE TO TELL ME." He laughed and said, "Where is it written that I <u>have</u> to tell you?" He was still laughing at me. I wasn't laughing. I wanted to know where we were going. He grabbed me around the waist and bent his head down to meet my face, kissed me and said, "We are going to ARUBA. How does that sound?" I couldn't talk. I just stared at him and I thought he was lying and still fooling around with me. "Vinnie, Tell me where we are really going?" He said, "I swear, we are going to Aruba." He picked me up and I wrapped my legs around him. He said, "I guess that means your happy about where we are going?" I just cried on his shoulder, then kissed him like I never kissed him before.

When we first met, we had a conversation about places we would like to go in our lifetime and mine was Aruba and his was the Bahamas. He was making my dream come true. He remembers everything I tell him. He

never forgets anything. Who made this guy?
Well, I mean, I know who made him, but really?
He was the best of the best and I don't think
there will be another one like him, ever, and he
was MINE.

We were off to Aruba and he had all kinds of
things planned and tours reserved. When did
he have time to do this? Maybe he did it while
I was sleeping? He is still amazing me. We
stayed at a gorgeous resort. We ate at a
million restaurants and saw every site and
went on tours and boat rides and sunset
cruises (romantic as hell) We saw Pink
Flamingo's, we went snorkeling and saw
Dolphins, we saw the beautiful Eagle Beach,
we went to a Butterfly Farm and we hit the
Wind Creek Seaport Casino and did a little
gambling and shopping. We had the best time
together. We went swimming at the resort in
the huge pool. We had a whirlpool tub in our
room and we used that too, many times… It
was the best vacation ever.

15

My settlement check had come while we were on our honeymoon and Vinnie was right (as usual). Attorney Castillo took $10,000 and my check was for $30,000. I made sure that I called him to let him know I received it and thanked him for all his help.

We got home with 1 day to spare before starting our new jobs. We unpacked and separated the clothes and we both washed, dried and folded clothes throughout the day. We ordered groceries for the week and got things to make quick meals just for this upcoming week. Next weekend, we could start the prepping again. We both contacted our parents to let them know we were back and safe and we told them that we would all get together and show them the million pictures we took.

We set out our clothes and our Jackets for work the next day and I sat on the bed staring at my jacket with my embroidered name.

"Renee Greco". Behind me I heard Vinnie say, "Hey, Mrs. Grecoooo?" I turned around and he smiled at me and we rolled around on the bed and made love for the second time today. I had a feeling there would be a few more times too.

The next morning we got up, showered and got dressed for our new jobs. Vinnie made coffee and I made some scrambled eggs, cheese and bacon sandwiches on a hard roll.

We grabbed our lunches out of the fridge and went to work. We were so excited to start in this office. We were greeted at the door by both doctors, who were grateful to see us. They shook our hands and welcomed us aboard and they asked us questions about our wedding and honeymoon. It was 7:45 and the office opened at 8:00.   I think they were glad that we were early. They showed us to our offices.

Vinnie and I were on opposite sides of the office, which was fine because it was easier to concentrate. We both got settled in and we got the breakdown of what was happening in the office today. We were introduced to the staff and we got our appointment book of patients for the day. Ms. Dr. Crowley's name was Evelyn and Mr. Dr. Crowley's name was Alex. Evelyn was super nice and very easy going and easy to work for. Our appointments were anywhere from 15 minutes to 45 minutes long. We had Telehealth calls as well and the nurses set them up for us. Most of those calls were eye infections, sore throats and sinus infections. If it was something more serious, the patients had to come into the office. Our first week was awesome and then we got into our schedule of home and work. After a couple weeks went by, we had Jimmie and Maria and his parents over for dinner and we showed them all our honeymoon pictures and told them about our jobs. I invited my parents and Rain's parents up for the weekend following that, and they were so excited to come. They took the train again and Vinnie picked them up at the train station. It was so much easier for them. They stayed Saturday and Saturday night and went home on Sunday.

***

16

A couple years went by and I got to experience all the snow that Upstate New York got. It was unbelievable. When it snowed up here, there was tons of it and it closed roads, businesses and stores. Vinnie and I were still loving our jobs. We had accumulated some vacation time and decided to take a couple weeks and go to Florida to sit in the warm summer sun and enjoy the beach during the winter months. The hard part was coming back to the snow after sitting on the beach.

Vinnie and I were laying in bed one night and he said, "Nay? Do you ever want to have kids?" I turned my head and smiled at him. "Of course I do. Are you ready for that phase?" He pulled me in for a hug and said, "I am so ready for that phase. I have been for a while, but all we do is work." I hugged him tight and said, "Well, I am ready. I am more than ready and I have been thinking a lot about it." He was so romantic and loving and he petted my head and smoothed my hair. "Let's do it. I was thinking 2 or 3? What do you think?" I said, "I was thinking, one at a time." And I laughed and I made him laugh. "Ah ha you are so fucking funny. I know that." I put my fingers through his hair and kissed his eyes and said, "2 or 3 is fine, but let's get one out of the way first." He said, "Ok, NOW?" I said, "YES NOW. But I took my birth control pill today and just so you don't get too excited, it doesn't happen right away ya know." He told me he was aware of that.

We tried and tried for 3 full months and nothing was happening, so we decided to make an appointment with my gynecologist first and see what was going on. She assured me that everything was fine and we just needed to relax and it will happen.

Another 3 months went by and nothing. Vinnie went and got tested to make sure there was nothing wrong with him and he was fine. His doctor told him to relax and it would happen.

We were relaxing and still nothing was happening, and I was getting depressed, so I told him I didn't want a baby and started crying. He felt so bad and said, "Ok, let's forget about it for a while. We are trying too hard. Let's give it a break."

Two months went by and I was late. I had a drawer full of tests and took one. Negative! I started crying in the bathroom and I felt like I was letting him down and I was a failure. I threw the test in the basket and straightened myself out and walked out. Fuck it. I don't care!

I was still late, but I didn't take a test right away because I just didn't want to feel bad anymore and I didn't feel like crying again. I waited and waited and I was still late. Now I was over a month late. Maybe I should take it again? I took another test out of the drawer and went into the bathroom.   I put the stick on the countertop and closed my eyes and covered them with my hands. I called for Vinnie, because I couldn't face another negative, alone. He knocked on the door and came in. "I can't be alone and see another negative". He knelt down in front of me and we both sat on the bathroom floor rug. He had his arm around me and hugged me while he held the stick and I kept my eyes covered. "Nay? Open your eyes babe. Open your eyes Nay." I peeked and he brushed my hands away from my eyes. "It's positive Nay. It's FUCKING POSITIVE NAY". I started crying instantly. How can it take almost a year to get pregnant? But it did and I didn't understand it. We were both so happy. He said, "We are gonna have a baby Nay. A baby."

He helped me get up off the floor and he said, "I think you should make an appointment with the Gynecologist and get the ball rolling and get on your prenatal vitamins. I will go with you to every single appointment. You will never be alone. I promise." I called on Monday and made my first appointment. They scheduled an ultrasound for 2 months, when we would find out the sex of the baby.

Apparently, the first test I took, was defective, because I was 2 months along. If only I had taken another test right away. But I was scared to see another negative, so I didn't do it. Vinnie and I were so proud and happy. He walked around with a permanent smile on his face. We still had one more month before we could tell anyone. He wanted to tell his brother first and I told him that parents are first and then siblings. He looked at me with a puzzled look and said, "There are rules for that?" I shook my head yes and said, "They are going to be Grandparents Vinnie, so yes, they are first to know. It just like, when I find out, I tell you first. How would you feel if I told someone else before you?" He said, "Oh Ok, I get it now. Yeah, I would be pretty upset if you told someone else before me." He paused and then said, "I know a great way to let them know. We wait for the ultrasound picture and then send them that, and a text that says, "Hi Grandma and Grandpa. I can't wait to meet you." I started laughing, "I love it Vinnie, and that will prompt the phone call and then we can talk to them." He said, "Do you want to send it to your parents first or mine?" I laughed and said, "We can send it at the same time. One from your phone and one from mine." He laughed and said, "Why didn't I think of that? I am so excited that I can't think straight anymore. Thank God it's Saturday."

I told him that if we wait for the ultrasound picture, that I would be 4 months, not 3, and he said he didn't care, because he wanted to tell our parents by sending the ultrasound picture.

He treated me like I was a piece of glass and I would break if I fell or got bruised. He always held my hand, or had his arm on my shoulder and he was always touching me in one way or another and I loved every minute.

It was ultrasound time and we were both so excited to see our little one and find out if we were having a girl or boy. Everything went according to plan and we found out we were having a little girl and we had a ton of pictures. Vinnie put his head on my belly and said, "I am waiting for you little one." The nurse got tears in her eyes and said, "That is so sweet. You made me tear up and I see this every day and I never do this." He said, "I think every guy should have a little girl first, because she will look like the woman that he fell in love with and then he will have two women that <u>caught his eye</u>." He winked at me and then bent over to kiss me.

The nurse congratulated both of us and Vinnie and I got our next appointment at the desk and we left.

He could not wait to send those texts to his parents and then his brother, and as soon as we got in the car, he took pictures of every single ultrasound picture. He attached the best picture we had and texted to his parents, "Hi Grammy and Papa, I can't wait to meet you, but you won't have too long to wait. I should be here around November 8." I told him to wait before sending, because I was gonna copy what he wrote and attach the same picture and we could send it at the same exact time. I copied what he said and he did the countdown and I was giggling. "3…2…1… GO".

Our friggin phones went bananas. His mother's phone, his father's phone, my mom's phone and my dad's phone, all went off almost immediately. They were all so excited and his mom said, "I was wondering when this was gonna happen. I started thinking you wouldn't have any." Vinnie explained what happened and that it took almost a year for me to get pregnant. My parents were also very excited and were saying similar things. Vinnie looked at me and said, "NOW?, Can I tell my brother now?" I smiled at him and said, "Yup go ahead. I am gonna tell Trevor and Mary now."

His mom kept texting and he told her we were still sitting in the car at the doctor's office and that we would call later, after dinner. Trevor and Mary responded first and they were so happy that we told them and that we were keeping them in the loop.

Jimmie and Maria were over the top happy for us and I think Jimmie was happier than anyone. He called Vinnie and kept saying, "OMG, WOAH, DUDE, I CAN'T WAIT. A LITTLE GIRL. OMG." He sent everyone a text saying that we were still at the doctor's office sitting in the car and that we would all have a FaceTime call later on after dinner. "I have to feed mommy before she passes out from hunger." He was chuckling to himself and then showed me what he wrote. I giggled and said, "Vinnie, that's not nice." He defended himself. "Babe, I am only kidding, but you _are_ feeding two." He paused and said, "I am taking you to The Water's Edge so we can have a really nice dinner. I hear they have awesome food there." I smiled and said, "I'm starving. I am in." He laughed and then started the car.

We sat in the booth and looked at the menu. I giggled to myself and said, "I will have a shot of tequila to start." He looked up from the menu and said, "In your dreams." I looked at him and said, "This place is a tease. I smell seafood and I want it." He said, "The doc said you can have it once in a while. Order away my love." So I did. I ordered a caffeine free coke and some fried calamari and a Filet Mignon with green beans and mashed potatoes and then a piece of carrot cake and I ate ALL of it. He smiled at me and said, "I knew you were hungry." I told him that everything was awesome and that we needed to come back to this place, next time I had a doctor's appointment. He agreed, so we made a date. I loved my dates with Vinnie. Our dates were anytime I got in the car with him. He always showed me a good time, a good dinner, or movie or mini golf. Anything I did with him, was a date, even a ride to the drugstore. He made it fun in one way or another. I love this guy with all my heart and soul and nobody was gonna change the feelings I had for him.

The last 5 months of my pregnancy were fine. I only had 2 incidents of being sick and those were in the first trimester. The rest of the time,

I just ate and got fat. The doctor said everything was going as planned and looked good and the baby was healthy and growing at a normal rate. She was very active and kicking all the time and Vinnie got such a kick out of it. Me, on the other hand, could have done with less of it because she was hurting me. I didn't mind the random kicks and movement, but near the end, she was in position and her feet were under my ribs when she kicked and it hurt like crazy.

When I was in my 8th month, Vinnie's parents and brother and sister-in-law invited my parents and Rain's parents up to their house and they gave us a baby shower. They went all out. It was at a restaurant and all Vinnie's relatives and family was there. They had a wishing well full of diapers in all sizes. We got so many cute little things. We got everything we needed for our baby girl. We got so many gifts that everyone had to put stuff in their car to get it back to our house. My parents and his parents talked all the time and kept in touch about what they were buying so we didn't get doubles, especially the furniture.

My mom and dad bought the crib and dressing table, Rain's parents bought the dresser and bassinet. Vinnie's parents also bought a bassinet so we would have one upstairs and downstairs and they bought tons of little dresses and hats and bows and a bathtub and a beautiful lamp and a mobile for the crib and diapers. I could go on and on with all the stuff we got.

Everyone kept asking us what we picked for a name. Vinnie wanted to wait till she was born, but I whispered to him at the shower that we should announce the name today.   Near the end of the shower, while everyone was having coffee and cake, he stood up and said, "Ok Everyone, first I want to thank everyone for coming and for all the beautiful gifts and for traveling to get here and second, we are going to tell you her name because everyone keeps asking." The place got super quiet. He laughed a little and said, "Her name is Lily Lorraine Greco." I thought Mary and Trevor were going to faint because we named her after Rain. They both started bawling, which made everyone else bawl, including me and we had a big bawl fest. Vinnie's mom got a little hysterical and that was because Lily was her mom's name. I told Vinnie that I needed to name her Lorraine for Trevor and Mary. It was the least I could do and it made me feel good. He had no problem with it at all, except he told me to never call her Rain. He wanted to name her after his maternal grandmother and I loved the name Lily.   It took us a while to pick this name, but I love it and was meant to be.

Jimmie and Maria came over with Kyle for a weekend and Jimmie helped Vinnie put together the furniture, except the crib. And they set up the room. Maria helped with washing all the clothes and hanging up the dresses and loading up the dresser with the onesies, bibs, hats and mittens. We loaded up the diapers in the holder and Vinnie put all the rest of the boxes in the closet. They set up the Camera/Monitor on the wall. They put together the highchair, but we left it in the spare room.

They put together both bassinets and put one in our bedroom and one downstairs in the living room. We had 2 car seats, one for each car and Jimmie showed Vinnie how to work them and they installed them in both our cars.

They put the stroller together and that was in the spare room. We had two little chairs that rocked. We literally did not have to buy one thing for our little girl. Not one thing.

I had my overnight bag packed and a pretty dress for Lily with all her necessities. Vinnie packed a bag too, because he promised me I would not be alone and he would always be there with me. Vinnie kept every promise he ever made to me. Every single one.

My due date came and went and I was a week late and looked like a roly poly, but the doctor said that everything was fine and it might have been a miscalculation on his part. I was thinking it was my fault because of the defective test I took and should have taken another one right away. Whatever it was, I was late. The doctor said that if I didn't go into labor by Friday that they would induce me on Saturday, and of course, I went into labor on Friday. It was a pretty easy delivery and I wasn't nervous at all. (All lies, don't believe it) Don't get me wrong, it hurt like a cannon ball going through a pin hole, but woman do it everyday and multiple times, so how hard could it be. LOL. Ha-ha. Yeah, I was screaming my brains out. Delaware heard me, because my mom was calling Vinnie and he hadn't told anyone. Of course, now she knew and spread the word and everyone was on pins and needles waiting for Lily to enter our world. Oh, she arrived and screamed her brains out before she was all the way out.

Vinnie took pictures and he cut the cord and had tears streaming down his face. He kissed me over and over and wiped my face with a cool cloth and told me how much he loved me and he said, "She caught my eye too Nay. She is beautiful, just like you." Lilly Lorraine Greco was 21 inches long and weighed 8lbs 10 oz and she had a full head of brown hair. She was such a gorgeous baby. Vinnie and I took turns holding her and the first one to the hospital to visit? Yup, his brother Jimmie and Maria and Kyle. Jimmie held her and kept saying she was the most beautiful baby girl he had ever seen. Vinnie's parents were the next to arrive and Rosa and Jay were fighting about who should hold her first. Rosa won and she held her for about 10 minutes and then Jay took her. They were in their glory and the smiles on their faces and the tears in their eyes were priceless.

I couldn't wait for my mom and dad to come and I am sure they were on their way as soon as they heard I was in labor. It was 5 hours after she had called Vinnie, so they should be here anytime now. Sure enough, they walked in the door with Mary and Trevor. My mom held her first and then my dad and then Mary and then Trevor. They all had the same look on their faces. It was a look of pure love. I don't think I will have any problems getting any help. LOL.

Vinnie gave Jimmie the key to our house and he got everyone situated. He built the crib with Jay, my dad (Daniel) and Trevor and everyone was all moved in for a few weeks. My mom (Susan) was cooking up a storm with Mary and

Rosa and making casseroles for during the week.

I was coming home today and Vinnie and I dressed Lily in the cute little dress and headband that I brought and wrapped her in a receiving blanket because it was freezing outside. We had a heavy blanket that we put over the carseat as he carried her out to the car (which was only a few feet). The car was warm and ready for her. I sat in the back with her and stared at her the whole time. She really was beautiful, but I bet all mothers think the same thing of their babies. 🩶

We pulled into the driveway and saw pink balloons on the mailbox and at the front door. We walked in and Vinnie was carrying Lily in her carseat and Jimmie came out to get the overnight bags and all the bottles and formula that the hospital gave us.

Lily was sleeping and Vinnie didn't want to wake her, so he put the little seat on the countertop so everyone could gawk at her. It would be feeding time in about an hour and I knew there would be fighting over her, so I told Vinnie that he should feed her.

He smiled at me and said, "Go sit down and relax. I will take care of it." Vinnie got a call from Evelyn and Alex Crowley, M.D.'s, congratulating us because Vinnie sent them a picture of Lily. We took maternity and paternity leave, so we were good for a few weeks.

The whole family ordered food from a restaurant nearby and had it delivered. They had a tray of Chicken Florentine , a tray of lasagna and a tray of lemon flounder in a butter sauce. There was garlic bread and hot rolls. The food was absolutely delicious. It was a place we never tried before but we would definitely be ordering from there again.

17

***

I was sitting in my recliner with the baby and looking out at the snow starting to fall and we had a small tree outside the window. I started to cry because Rain came to say HI. She was sitting on the branch out there, looking into the window. It could have been any bird, but that bird flew to the window and was sitting on the outside sill and just staring at me and the baby. It was definitely Rain. I waved to her and she flew away. I dried my tears and told Vinnie. "Rain came to visit me today. She sat right on the sill outside the window. I waved to her and then she flew away." He hugged me. "She was thanking you for naming the baby after her."

Little Miss Lily was an absolute angel. She was a really good baby. She cried when she was hungry or had gas, but as soon as those problems were resolved, she was smiling, laughing and goo gooing. She had Vinnie's eyes and the rest was me, well, except for his double toes. He had two toes on each foot that were connected, like a web and his brother had the same thing. No one knows where it came from because his mom and dad did not have it and Kyle didn't get it either.

Vinnie's paternity leave was over, but I still had 3 months. My mom and dad stayed to help me and everyone else went home. I had to find daycare, but I was scared to trust anyone with her. My mom offered, but she lived too far away. Maria offered to do it for a while and I trusted her completely, but she had her hands full with Kyle and I think she was pregnant, although there was no announcement yet.

Vinnie came home for lunch every single day, because the office was 3 minutes down the road. It was killing him not to be with us and I knew that, but there was nothing I could do. He discussed with me the possibility of me not going back to work. I looked at him shocked. "You want me to stay home?" He said, "I am not telling you what to do. I am merely giving you a choice. If you want to stay home and take care of Lily, you can. We are fine money wise and we make a lot of money now. Maybe you could take a Leave of Absence and think on it for a while? Or if you know what you want to do, just do it. Whatever you want to do Nay." I smiled at him and said, "I want to stay home and take care of Lily. I don't think I can leave her." He hugged me and said, "I am happy with your decision. Really happy. But I know two people that won't be happy. Evelyn and Alex Crowley. Ev really likes you and the patients really like you. Maybe down the road, when the kids get bigger and go to school, you can go back, but only if you want to." I smiled at him and said, "KIDS?" He laughed and said, "Well, we are having more, aren't we? And I don't want to wait, like years. I wanna have them pretty close together.

We can talk about this another time because Lily is only 3 months. I laughed and said, "Ok, we will talk tonight." I gave him his lunch and he held Lily while he was eating it.

I had my 3 month checkup with my gynecologist and he said I was good to go, but he told me to be careful, because I could get pregnant, like that and he snapped his fingers.

I laughed and said, "Yeah right. It took me almost a year with Lily." He said, "Renee, I am warning you, you can get pregnant very easily right now. You are very fertile after having a baby." I shrugged it off and went home.

I told Vinnie what he said and he laughed too. He was happy that the doctor cleared me, because normally it is 6 weeks and then you can have sex, but he told us to wait because of some issue that I can't explain. Vinnie didn't waste anytime and that night we went at it, like rabbits, when Lily was sleeping.

Well, the doctor was right. I was fucking fertile as hell, because I was pregnant. I took a test and couldn't believe it was positive. Vinnie came home for lunch and I showed him the stick. He opened his mouth in shock. "What the fuck? OMG. Do you know what this means?" I shook my head no. "It means we are having Irish twins. Lily Bear will be one year old, when this baby is born. Holy Shit Nay. This is fucking great." I laughed and said, "Well, I guess we don't have to discuss it then." He busted out laughing and picked me up to swing me around and he was kissing me.

He said, "I am soooo soooo happy. You have no idea, no idea whatsoever." I kissed him and said, "Yes, yes, I think I do. Do NOT tell anyone about this yet. No one, not even Jimmie." He promised that he wouldn't, so I trusted him.

I called my gynecologist's office and told them and my doctor called me back and when I answered, he laughed and said, "I told you Renee. What do you need? Are you keeping the baby?" I was shocked at that question. I was quiet. "Yes, yes, of course, I am keeping the baby. What kind of question is that? Vinnie and I are planning on having 2-3 kids total and we want them close together, although we didn't plan on this close, we _are_ happy about it." He told me that he didn't mean anything by that question and made an appointment for us to come in and confirm the pregnancy and he would prescribe my vitamins.

Vinnie and I took Lily Bear and went to my first appointment and Dr. Nussear was happy to see her. "She is getting so big already. She is

3 months now?" Vinnie told him she was 3 months and that he was looking forward to our new baby. Lily Bear's hair turned blondish and I think we may have a blondie in the family. He smiled at Vinnie and said, "Irish twins. You will have your hands full." Vinnie smiled back and said, "I am looking forward to it." The doctor confirmed my pregnancy and gave us a due date of November 15th, which was Lily's First Birthday."

We told everyone about this pregnancy, the same as we did last time. We waited for the ultrasound and found out we were having a boy this time. We got a different response to this pregnancy this time around. Everyone was shocked to find out that I was pregnant again so soon. My mom thought it was too soon and asked if it was dangerous and she was just being concerned and I told her I was fine and the doctor didn't seem concerned at all and that people do it all the time. Rosa and Jay had the same concern, but Jimmie was so excited for us. He was a baby lover and he called when he got the text. "DUDE THIS IS

FUCKING AWESOME. I AM SO HAPPY FOR YOU." Vinnie looked at me and said, "Well, I am glad one person is happy about it." I looked at him and said, "Everyone is happy Vinnie, they are just concerned that it is too soon. And for the record, I am super happy, and personally, it's no one's business, but ours." He picked me up and hugged me. "I love the fuck out of you Nay and I always will and I am super fucking happy about this baby."

Marie was pregnant, when I thought she was, but she lost the baby in the first trimester. Jimmie told Vinnie about it, but no one else in the family, except us, knew about it. Jimmie was crushed and we went to visit and console them. They are still trying for another one and I told Maria that it will happen and told her my story about Lily.

***

This pregnancy was totally different from Lily's. I was sick for 5 months and couldn't hold any food down. I was hungry, but as soon as I finished eating, it came right back up. I was losing weight instead of gaining it. The doctor had to give me something to settle everything down and after month 5 it was better. My hormones were crazy with this pregnancy and I cried for 9 months about nothing. I was eating pickles and whipped cream, I was mixing weird foods together and I was craving hot fudge sundaes. I was getting up in the middle of the night to eat Fritos with dip and cereal. I was starving and gaining weight like crazy. The doctor was concerned because I gained 40 pounds and I still had 2 months to go, when the baby puts on weight.

Vinnie took me to the Water's Edge restaurant once a month when we had our doctor's appointment and Lily Bear was such a good girl, while Mommy ate whatever was assessable to her and became a big fat pig. I got out of the shower one night and looked in the mirror and started crying. Vinnie heard me and came in. "What's wrong babe? Are you ok?" I told him I was a big fat pig and I was ugly and he wouldn't want me anymore and he wouldn't find me pretty anymore. He hugged me and said, "You are the most beautiful girl I ever laid my eyes on and I will love you no matter what. You are pregnant and so you WILL gain weight. All pregnancies are different babe. Stop worrying about what you look like. I love the shit out of you and always will, no matter what. You caught my eye many years ago and you still catch my eye every time I see you." He hugged me from behind and rubbed my big fat belly and he had his head on my shoulder. He said, "Look at that babe. It's fucking amazing. It's a miracle! You are growing another baby in there. It's not all fat, it's a big baby."

Vinnie was rocking Lily Bear and giving her, her last bottle before bed. I went into the closet and got my plush pink robe out because I was a little chilly and noticed the box that Mary had given me so long ago after Rain had died. Should I take it out and see what else is in it? I want to, but I don't want to get upset again. I really should know what she wanted to give me or tell me. I pulled it out and sat in the rocking chair in our bedroom. I pulled out a few things that I had given her that she cherished and I put them back in the box. The only thing left was a sealed envelope in the bottom of the box. My name was on it, printed in neat handwriting, "RENEE". I opened it and started reading it.

Dear Nay:

I want you to know how much I really loved you. As a friend, of course. What I have to tell you, stays between us forever. Do not ever tell my parents, especially my mom, because it will break their hearts. I was pregnant with Jason's baby and I aborted it, because I found out that I had breast cancer. Jason knew about the baby, but not the cancer and I told him that I miscarried. They found the cancer when I went for my mammogram. My mom would freak out, because that is what my grandma died of. Please Nay, do not tell her, because I know that she is already suffering because of my decision to commit suicide. I did this to save everyone, including you, from feeling sorry for me. You know me better than anyone and you know I hate that shit. I did not want people feeling sorry for me or worrying about me. This was a quicker way and I would not suffer either. That day that I put my coffee on the table and sipped it without picking it up, was the morning, I aborted the baby and I was really weak and I knew you were only fooling around with me, but I was miserable. I apologize for any wrong doing to you, because you were my BFF and you know that. I will visit you in the tree outside your window. I will be the red cardinal in the snow.

Love you always,

RAIN

I sat there and cried for an hour after reading this letter. It was Rain in the tree outside my window in the snow, It WAS!! Because how would she know I had a tree outside my window? How did she know it would be snowing? I will always look out there for her, for the rest of my life. Vinnie had peaked in on me, while I was reading the letter, but he just backed out and left me alone to deal with it and I was glad. I folded the letter and put it back in the envelope and put the envelope in the box and put the box back in the closet. I saw everything in the box and now I was done. I would never tell Mary or Trevor, because I was under oath and she knew she could trust me. I did tell Vinnie though and then he felt bad. I told him about the cardinal in the tree in the snow and he believed it was Rain too. We both felt bad. You never know what someone has on their plate or what they are suffering with. She could have told me, but she never liked anyone feeling sorry for her for any reason, not even me, and that is why she never said a word to me.

I had one month to go and the weight gain had evened out and I wasn't putting it on like I was before. I am surprised though, because my appetite was the same. I ate everything in site and anything I craved, Vinnie got it. He said that it was important to eat what I craved because that meant that my body or the baby wanted it. Yeah, I call bullshit on that. My brain wanted it, not my body or the baby. This shit of eating for 24 hours a day was gonna stop and I would get back to normal as soon as possible. I was so uncomfortable and I was waddling around. My mom and dad came with Mary and Trevor and they stayed at the house and they helped with Lily and they would be here when I went into labor.

Vinnie got a call from Jimmie a week later and he told us that Maria was 4 months pregnant with a little girl and they were so excited, as they should be. Vinnie's parents came to visit on Sunday November 14th and Vinnie invited his brother and family too and we ordered a bunch of food from that restaurant down the street. Oh that made fatso happy because I just used a shovel and ate everything in site. It was November 14th and we were planning on a birthday party for Lily tomorrow. Vinnie ordered the cake and the food, but I had a different agenda.

My water broke after dinner on the 14th and I went into labor. Vinnie and I left everyone at the house and they assured us that Lily Bear would be well taken care of. My labor was really bad for this baby and I screamed for hours and then they gave me an epidural. James Vincent Greco was born at 3:00 a.m. on November 15th. He was 9lbs, 10 oz. He was 22 inches long and had a full head of brown hair like Lily. He was a big boy with fat cheeks and he had my eyes, but he had his daddy's lips and nose and he looked exactly like Vinnie. Our whole family showed up with Lily around noon the next day and they brought the food and cake and even a couple of balloons and we had Miss Lily Bear's birthday party at the hospital. They got permission from the hospital I guess, because no one said a word. We invited our nurses to eat and have cake, too. Lily Bear got to meet her Irish twin brother and she just stared at him. Jimmie teared up because we named him after him. Vinnie loved his brother so much and said he owed it to him. He got no complaints out of me. AND, James Vincent had webbed toes too. Where did this trait come from? Rosa and Jay inspected their Grandson for that when they got there and started laughing when they found it.

We celebrated two birthdays in the hospital. I was really sore with this birth because he was a huge baby to push out and I had stitches. I was tired and started dozing off after I ate lunch. I kissed my little Lily Bear before she left and I don't remember anything after that. I was out like a light. Vinnie stayed and took care of the baby and was with me the whole time. He never left my side for a minute. I slept for a while and when I woke up, Vinnie was sitting in the chair feeding the baby. He was such a natural with babies. Everything was all cleaned up and they left us two plates of food and 2 pieces of birthday cake and they left the balloons floating around the room. Vinnie finished feeding and burping and Little James was fast asleep so he put him in his little hospital bassinet and rewrapped him in the receiving blanket. He came over to me, because I was smiling at him and he bent over and kissed me. "Thank you for my son." I told him, that he is the one that determines whether it is a boy or girl and he said, "Yes, I know, but you gave birth to him. He is a beautiful little boy, Nay. We make beautiful babies." He kissed me on my forehead and left his lips there for a long time. I said, "I can't believe they have the same birthday. That is amazing." He smiled and said, "It will make it easier on us for birthday parties. One party and done. Well, until they get older."

Doctor Nussear came in to see us and told me that he was releasing me to go home tomorrow afternoon and everything looked good. James (Jamie) was going to be circumcised in the morning and he was checked out by the pediatrician and he is healthy as an ox.

We got home the next day and our whole family was waiting for us. Jimmie was right there getting our bags out of the car and

Vinnie carried the baby in his carseat. Maria came out to help me into the house. Shit, I was so sore and I walked like I had a bowling ball between my legs. I had stitches this time around but I didn't have that with Lily. The first thing I did was go to the bathroom and then I got into my recliner near the window.

We just made it home and it started to snow. I looked out on the tree branch and waited for Rain to visit. She wasn't there yet, but I knew she would be coming to welcome James Vincent Greco. I really believed that letter she wrote, because I had already seen her before reading it. Vinnie handed me Little James and a bottle and I started to feed him and looked out the window and there she was. I nudged Vinnie and pointed. Mary came over and said, "What's out there?" I had no qualms about telling her what I thought and I told her. "Rain is visiting us and she is welcoming Mr. James. See her?" Mary surprised the shit out of me and said, "Yes, she visits me too. She told me in a letter that she would be visiting in the bush next to my bedroom window and I have seen her twice already." I touched her arm and said, "She told me in my letter that she would be visiting in this tree. How would she know that? She didn't even know where I lived, but I guess she does now." Mary was at peace with Rain's death and she didn't even shed a tear and Trevor told me later that she was on medication for depression and she was 100% better. I was happy about that. I guess I was at peace too, but I still shed tears every time I think about her.

18

Maria and Jimmy were patiently awaiting their little girl and they were thinking of names. Maria wanted her first name to be after her grandma, Ruthie and Jimmie got to pick the middle name and he picked Renee. I was shocked and said to Jimmie, "I am so honored. Thank you so much." So her name was going to be Ruthie Renee Greco. Vinnie and I loved the name and Maria's parents were so happy that they named her after her maternal grandma.

Maria had 1 month to go and I told Vinnie that we should give her a little shower because of all the things they have done for us. We reached out to Rosa and Jay and we set it up and I invited my mom and dad and Mary and Trevor too. We had it at a restaurant and Vinnie and I decorated. We wanted to surprise them, so I put all of Lily's clothes that didn't fit her anymore, into a box and used that as an excuse to visit. Vinnie carried the box in and held Lily's hand and I carried Little James. Vinnie said, "We brought you a shitload of clothes that don't fit Lily anymore and thought you could use them." Maria was so happy about that. We went near dinner time and it was perfect because they were gonna order out. Vinnie said, "Let go out to the restaurant in town. He looked at me and said, "What's the name of it babe?" I spoke up and said, "I think it's called the windmill or something." Jimmie said, "Yeah, that sounds good. Let's go." They put shoes on Kyle and got ready. When we got there, we made them walk in first and everyone yelled surprise.

They were both surprised. Jimmie looked at his brother and said, "Yeah, what's the name of that restaurant babe? Ha ha, you really pulled it off." Vinnie laughed and said, "Well, you fell for it, sooo…. We all ordered dinner and did a lot of talking and Vinnie and I were passing Little James around so everyone could hold him and Lily Bear made her rounds to all the grandma's, including Mary. She was considered Grandma Mary and that made her very, very happy. She ended up sitting in my dad's lap. She loved him so much and then she got down and went to Papa Jay, who she also adored. I think it was because they gave her whatever she wanted, even if we said no.

Jimmie and Maria opened all their gifts and we made sure they had everything they needed. Kyle was 3, almost 4, so they needed all new stuff. The grandparents bought them the new furniture, crib, dresser and dressing table. We bought them a bassinet and diapers and onesies and dresses and headbands and bows and sneakers and booties and bibs. Vinnie and I went crazy when we went shopping. They got a monitor from Mary and Trevor, along with clothes and diapers and a cute little dress with a matching sunhat. They didn't need anything for the new baby and we made sure of it.

Jimmie had his parents stay at the house with him and help him with Kyle until Maria went into labor. It's a good thing he did because Maria went into labor 2 1/2 weeks early. She had a hard delivery and they almost had to do a cesarean, but Ruthie turned last minute and she saved her mom from a lot of pain. She was 20 inches long with light, light brown hair and she weighed 6 lbs. 2 oz. She was a little peanut and that is what I nicknamed her 'My little peanut.' Vinnie and I went to visit and Lily Bear was fascinated by her. Little James could care less. He was playing with the zipper on my coat. He was easy to amuse and he was a quiet baby. Lily Bear tried to crawl up in bed with Maria, but Vinnie stopped her. Maria wanted her to come up, so Vinnie picked her up and placed her next to Maria, who put her arm around her and Lily snuggled right in next to her. She loves her Onnie MeAH.

Vinnie is the one who gave her the nick name of Lily Bear. He loves her with all his heart. He tells everyone that she is the 'apple of his eye'. If someone calls her Lily, she looks at them and says, 'Bear'. Lily Bear turned out to be a little blondie and I have no idea where it came from. I have brown hair and Vinnie has dark brown. No one on his side or my side has blonde hair.   She has blue eyes and Vinnie and I have greenish eyes, but my mom said that my grandma had blueish eyes.

Jamie still has light brown hair and blue eyes, but he is only 3 months, so his eyes may still change. He loves his big sister and she adores him and plays with him all the time. She is very gentle with him, but Vinnie keeps a close eye on her. We let her hold him on the couch and she giggles at him and he smiles back at her and we have some great pictures of that.

They are heart tugging pictures and my parents and Vinnie's parents always get teary eyed when we show them.

19

***

I was busy getting Lily Bear some lunch and warming up some baby food for Jamie, when my phone rang. I put it on speaker, so I could continue what I was doing. "Hello?" My mom's voice was on the other end. "Hi Honey. I hope I am not interrupting you." I said, "No mom, I have you on speaker. I am warming up baby food and making lunch for Lily Bear. What's up? Is everything ok?" She was chuckling on the other end. "I am interrupting you." I laughed and said, "This is my life now mom. Everyday, all day." She said, "I have some really good news for you. Sit down." I was puzzled and lowered my eyebrows. What could she be telling me that was so good, that I needed to sit down? She said, "Ya ready?" She knows I hate when she does this.

"MOM?" She laughed and said, "We sold our house and Mary and Trevor sold their house. We bought a duplex together, in Upstate New

York, right near your house." I stood up in shock and yelled. "WHAT? WHAT? ARE YOU KIDDING? OMG MOM. YOU DON'T KNOW HOW HAPPY THIS MAKES ME. IS THIS A FUCKING JOKE MA?" She assured me that it was not a joke. They went halves on the duplex and they would be living next-door to each other and they were only 2 miles away from us. It took me all afternoon to get it through my head that my mom and dad and Mary and Trevor were going to live near us. I couldn't wait to tell Vinnie when he got home.

I put the kids down for their naps and kept texting my mom. She told me that they sold their houses furnished and they were only taking their personal belongings and their TV's and stuff, but the living room and bedrooms and dressers and kitchen table and chairs were staying. They bought the duplex and they were paying for it with the proceeds from the houses and they were going to buy all new furniture. She told me that they needed a place to stay for a week while they waited for the closing and to have the furniture delivered. I told her that they could stay as long as they needed. She told me they had to be out of the house in 2 weeks and I asked if she needed help and she said, "No, we did some packing and we hired someone to come and do the rest. Mary and Trevor did the same. We are all set and I am so excited."

I started dinner and Lily Bear was playing in her playpen and Jamie was in his chair on the counter and I was rocking him here and there as I was dicing vegetables for soup tomorrow. Tonight was meatloaf, mashed potatoes and baby peas. Lily Bear loved this dinner and believe it or not, she loved the peas. But that was because Vinnie would throw them in her dish and then make believe it wasn't him. She would look around and wonder where they came from and we would snicker under our breaths, but she ate every single one. She ate everything I made and she wasn't fussy at all. She loved food, like her mama.

I was good though and I lost all my baby weight. I was strict with myself because I was uncomfortable being heavy. I had gained 15 pounds with Little Jamie and it was gone. I had stretch marks up the ying yang, but I was putting some magic cream on them to make them go away. I doubt it would work, but it was worth a try. I didn't care if they didn't go away because that was part of being a mother and I was proud to be one.

Vinnie and I decided that two children was enough. We had a boy and a girl and we were happy with that. Jimmie and Maria also decided that 2 was enough, so there would be no more babies in this family. Vinnie went for a vasectomy, so we were sure we were not having anymore. He wasn't happy when he came home, but ice packs helped and a couple of days later, he was fine.

He was still working with Evelyn and Alex and Evelyn hired another Physician's Assistant. I felt bad that I left, but family comes first and I gave her a good 4 years before I left. She calls me once in a while to see how everything is going and Vinnie and I brought the kids in a few times. If you could see his face when we go places with them…He is so proud of his kids and it shows on his face and in his eyes. He loves showing them off and talking about them.

Vinnie got home from work and I told him that everyone was moving up here and he just smiled and said, "I know." I looked at him and said, "What do you mean, you know?" He laughed. He said, "Sorry babe. They wanted to surprise you, but they needed help with some stuff, so I helped them and they made me swear not to tell you." I said, "Wow, you really can keep a secret, because I had no fucking idea what was going on until my mom called me today. She told me to sit down and I almost fell off the chair." He laughed. "Are you happy?" I said, "Of course I am happy and you should be too. No more picking everyone up at the train station." He chuckled and said, "That didn't bother me, but now at least they can see the kids all the time and you will be close to them. I know it kills you to be so far away from them." I told him I couldn't wait for them to get here. He told me that he hired some people to help them move and pack and get here safe. He said, "I am shipping their cars here and they are taking the train one last time." The moving truck will have your mom and dad's stuff and also Mary and Trevor's stuff. The duplex is really nice and spacious and perfect for them. I looked at it with them and helped them with the lawyer and deposit. I looked at him and said, "WHAT? They were here and you went with them to look at it? Really??" He looked upset. "I'm sorry babe. It's what they wanted, so I tried to please them. I picked them up from the train station, took them to see it, helped them with the paperwork, took them back to the train station and went back to work." He had his head down, like a kid that did something bad. I laughed. "You are something else, Mr. Greco. I love you so fucking much. I can't believe you did all this to please me." He smiled and felt better. "I told you, you caught my eye and I would do anything for you. You are the love of my life." He hugged me tight and kissed me and Lily Bear wanted to get in on the action, so he picked her up and we had a group hug. I bent down to Jamie and hugged him too. I said, "So when is all this happening. My mom never gave me a date or maybe she did and I was so excited that I didn't hear her." He laughed and said, "In 2 weeks on Friday."

I looked on my phone calendar and put it in. He said, "Don't worry about cleaning the bedrooms and all that. I hired a housekeeper/ maid for a month and she will be here everyday. They will clean everything before they come and while they are here and after

they leave. You have enough on your plate
with the kids and I want you to enjoy the
company while they are here." I was happy
about that because I really _did_ have my hands
full. I said, "Vinnie, Are you taking any
vacation time during this event?" He laughed
and said, "Yeah, I think I will. I will tell Alex
tomorrow."

We sat down to eat dinner and Vinnie heated
up the baby food and bottle and I cut
everything up for Lily Bear and gave her a
sippy cup of milk. He loved feeding Jamie and
played airplane with him. That child did not
need any coaxing to eat at all. He had a good
appetite, all the time, but Vinnie loved to see
him smile as the spoon was coming towards
his mouth. He did the same thing with Lily,
when she was that age.

I started thinking that I wanted to fulfill Vinnie's
dream of going to the Bahamas, but it was still
too early to leave the kids with grandparents
for a week. I think that I will do it when Jamie
is one year old and Lily Bear is 2. They can all
take turns taking care of them. I want him to
have his dream too. He gave me mine, so it's
only fair, right? I want to surprise him like he

surprised me. I talked to my mom and dad and Vinnie's mom and dad and asked them what they thought about watching the kids for a week when Jamie was a year old. I told them I wanted it to be a surprise. They said yes, of course. I talked to Dr. Alex and set it up with him, so he knew what week he would be taking off and he was willing to play along with me and make it a surprise.

I set it up for the week after the kid's birthdays in November. I made the plane reservations and resort reservations and got a package deal, which was very reasonable. I let everyone know when it was and we were all set. I was excited and now I just had to wait 6 months and keep it a secret at the same time. I told Jimmie and Maria and Jimmie told me that he has always talked about going there and he was pleased with me. "You are a good wife Renee. He couldn't have done any better than you." I said, "Aww. Jimmie, thanks. You did a good job too with Maria. You are one lucky son of a bitch." He laughed and said, "You got that right. He is gonna be so happy, Nay. Me and Maria will help out if needed too, so don't worry about anything. Ok?" I thanked him.

20

***

The day finally came when my mom, dad, Mary and Trevor moved up here and everything went according to plan. They stayed with us for a week, after their closing and they were waiting for furniture deliveries. They unpacked kitchen boxes and bathroom boxes and put their clothes in the closets but that is all they could do until the furniture came.

They bought all their furniture at the same store so they were only waiting for one delivery for both places. The furniture was delivered and Vinnie and Jimmie helped them move in, along with his mom and dad. Maria and I were too busy with the kids, so we stayed home and out of the way. In less than a week, they had everything unpacked and they moved out of our house into their own. It was gonna be so nice having them so close to us.

Six months flew by and we had a Birthday party for Jamie and Lily Bear. It was cold and snowy, so it was inside and it was just family, The Crowleys and Rain's parents.

The following week was my surprise to Vinnie. I left him a note in the bathroom on Friday night while he was taking a shower.

To my love:

You are on vacation for one week and I am taking you to a very special place. We are leaving on Sunday morning at 6:00 a.m. I removed your suitcase from the closet and I want you to pack it with things you will need on a beach and something to go out to dinner in. Everything is taken care of. The kids have 3 sets of grandparents and an Aunt and Uncle who love them dearly and they will be well taken care of. The Crowleys put in for your vacation and we are ready to go.

You caught my eye too,

Love

Nay

XOXO

He came out of the shower with the letter and a towel wrapped around him and the biggest smile on his face. "Nay? Where are we going?" I said, "It's a surprise." He said, "You have to tell me Nay." I laughed and said, "Where is it written that I have to tell you?" He said, "He he he. OMG, you think you are so smart, don't you. That is what I said to you." I laughed and said, "Ah ha, you remember?" He started chasing me around and kept saying, "WHERE ARE WE GOING NAY? WHERE ARE WE GOING NAY?" I caved and said, "I am taking you to…" and I stopped. He said, "You are fucking killing me. WHERE?" "The Bahamas babe. The Bahamas". He opened his mouth in shock and said, "ARE YOU FUCKING KIDDING ME? REALLY? I ALWAYS WANTED TO GO THERE MY WHOLE LIFE."   I said, "Remember when we met and we told each other where we wanted to go? Mine was Aruba and you made that dream come true for me. Yours was The Bahamas and I am making your dream come true too." He said, "I can't believe you did this. I really can't believe it. We have plane tickets and hotel and everything?" I shook my head and showed him the itinerary. I said, "I had to keep this a secret for 6 months. Do you know how hard that was?" He laughed. "Really hard for you, Nay."

He was all excited and put the suitcase on the bed and threw in all his bathing suits. I think he has about 6. He threw in some dress clothes and shorts and t-shirts and his shower stuff and his brush, etc. He closed it up an hour later and said, "I am fucking ready to ROCK."

We left on Sunday, early morning, and kissed our babies. My mom and dad were staying at our house, along with Grandma Mary and Papa Trevor. We were staying at THE ROYAL at Atlantis. I bought the all inclusive Couples Getaway package and we had daily access to the Water Park, Shuttle service, we got one free dinner credit for any restaurant we wanted and Daily Breakfast for 2 and this was for the first 3 days and nights. Then we were going to Nassau Atlantis Paradise Island.

I had tours planned and reservations at beautiful restaurants and sightseeing Jeep tours. We did a Pirate's Gold Nassau Scavenger Hunt Adventure, we did a Jet Ski

Adventure in Cabbage Beach and a Snorkel Tour on Rose Island. We saw the swimming pigs, which is like a main attraction, but that did not turn me on at all. Vinnie liked it and this was his dream, so we did it. We did a swimming with the turtles adventure and a Sunset Dinner Cruise in Nassau.

We also did a lot of beach days and water walking. Vinnie was in his glory and kept taking selfies of both of us and sending to everyone. We spent a total of 6 days and 6 nights and we were on our way home. He kissed me and hugged me and was so grateful that I did this for him and it made me feel good that I could give him something that he wanted.

Now we were on our way back to a snow storm and we prayed that there wouldn't be a delay. We kept checking to make sure we were not delayed and we ended up being fine, but I was scared when it came to landing. It was snowing hard and the runway kept getting covered, but they salted I guess, or whatever they do to keep it clear and we were fine. We put on our winter coats, but we didn't have boots. Oh well, we would be fine. Frozen, but fine.

We had a limo ride home and it was slow going, but we made it and everyone was in the picture window waiting for us. Mary was holding Jamie and my mom was holding Lily Bear. Jimmie was outside shoveling the driveway to keep it clear for us. The limo driver pulled right into the driveway and Vinnie tipped him big because of the snow. We got out and Jimmie opened the garage door and came to help with the luggage and we walked right in. Who needs boots when you have a sweet brother-in-law? We hugged him and thanked him for shoveling to keep it clean for us.

We unpacked one suitcase that we had packed with trinkets for everyone and we all sat in the living room as Vinnie passed them out. LilyBear and Jamie got snow globes for their rooms. It was a beach with shells and a palm tree and flowers and footprints. We bought T-shirts and sweatshirts for his Dad, my Dad, Trevor and Jimmie. Vinnie bought Jimmie a shot glass and a coffee cup too. I bought Maria a hoodie sweatshirt and a coffee mug. I bought my mom and Mary sweatshirts and mugs and I got my mom a Sea Turtle wind chime. Mary, Mom and Maria also got Refrigerator magnets. Vinnie bought The Crowleys a couple of sweatshirts and coffee mugs.

While we were on vacation and looking through the gift shops, I spotted a Red Cardinal sitting on top of a wind chime and it had a black metal oval at the bottom that made them ring. On the black oval, it said, "Cardinals appear when angels are near". I bought two of them, one for Mary and one for myself. I gave it to Mary and told her to hang it near the bush where Rain appears and I was going to hang mine in the window outside where I saw her near the tree. She teared up, but she was ok and hugged me tight and thanked me. She said, "You always get the most thoughtful gifts. I love you with all my heart." I hugged her and said, "I love you too Mary."

I had Jamie in my lap and Daddy had his little Lily Bear in his lap and they were so happy to see us. Lily was all tucked into her Daddy's arm and hugging him. Jamie was doing the same to me and he was almost pinching me, he was holding me so tight. They were very clingy for about a week. They both just wanted to be held all day. Vinnie had to go back to work, but he made sure he came home at lunch and LilyBear was right there waiting for him at the door. She was so attached to him and Jamie was more attached to me. They go through phases, I guess, because before we left, it was the other way around.

21

Jamie was walking now, actually running, and he was a handful and getting into everything. It was so bad, that I had to coral him in the playpen, full of toys, for most of the day, so I could get laundry and cooking done. He was happy, but I felt bad that he couldn't be free. I didn't have this problem with Lily Bear because when I said, "Don't touch", she listened, amazingly enough. She looked at me, lifted her hand off the object and then smiled at me. Jamie, on the other hand, was totally different. If I said, "Don't touch", he picked up the object and started running with it. Little shit. LOL. He made me laugh many times, when I shouldn't have, because then it became a game, but I solved it by putting him in his playpen. It was a big playpen and Lily wanted to go in it with him, and play, and that was fine with me. He didn't cry at all and actually loved being in it, especially when his sister joined him. I am glad we stopped at two children, because they were a handful all day. One of each was fine with me and Vinnie agreed. He always says, "One for each lap. What would we do with 3?" I was so happy when he got home from work, because he spent time with them and they got out of the playpen for a while. He usually changed their diapers and got them a juice box and sat them both in his lap and watched cartoons with them, until dinner. After dinner, I would clear the table and put the dishes in the dishwasher and he cleaned the kids up with a washcloth and cleaned their highchairs. Then he would clean off the dining room table, come in and give me kisses from behind, while I was washing the pots and pans. He dried and I went to get the kids and I got to spend time with them before bath time and bed.

I filled the bathtub and we both gave them a bath at the same time. I would be on one side and Vinnie on the other side and we each washed a child. We had it down to a science. He had a towel and I had a towel and we wrapped them and brought them into their bedroom and got them in their PJ's with clean diapers.

They were allowed to play and watch TV in the living room for a couple hours and then they both had a bottle, another diaper change and off to bed. They had a schedule and they were used to it. Children need schedules for sleeping, playing and eating because it helps them learn discipline. Vinnie and I were strict to the schedules because it helped us too.

I was so tired at night, that I usually fell asleep sitting up watching TV, so I made sure I showered and got in my nightgown before that happened. I actually fell asleep while I was folding clothes one night. Vinnie went in to take a shower and when he came out he found me sleeping with a folded towel in my hand. He carried me to bed and finished folding the clothes. This is one of the reasons I love this man so much.

Jimmie and Maria did the same with schedules and it worked for them as well. My mom used to get mad when she came to visit and they had to go down for a nap, but she knew we were on a strict schedule. I used to tell her that if I didn't put them down for a nap, that she could take them home and take care of them and it wouldn't be fun.

It was almost birthday time again. Jamie would be two and Lily Bear was going to be three. We planned on having the party on their birthday, but the weather had other plans for us. We were expecting a blizzard. This was the first one I would ever experience since living here and didn't know what to expect. We had their birthday party 2 days before their birthday and everyone came to celebrate and the kids were all excited. Mostly to see their grandma's and papa's. Lily Bear took turns sitting in everyone's lap. She was a little lover girl and always snuggled right into everyone.

She knew how to wrap you around her pinky finger to get what she wanted. She kept asking for cake before dinner and Vinnie and I both told her she had to wait, but Papa Greco dipped his finger in the cake and gave her some and then she went to Papa Madden and he did the same. She made the rounds and Papa Trevor did it too, but he got caught by Daddy Vinnie. We all just laughed because she was so smart and she knew what she was doing. We ordered trays of food and a sheet cake with a line down the middle. Each side had their names on it and we sang Happy Birthday to Lily Bear, one side of the cake and then lit the candles on the other side and sang Happy Birthday to Jamie.

We were all discussing the upcoming Blizzard and I wondered if anyone had experienced one before. Vinnie and I never went through one before. Jimmie asked if we had wood and we did, but not a lot. He told us that would be our heat and it's important to have a lot of it. He texted the guy that he usually gets it from and ordered a cord for us. He would deliver it tomorrow. He told Vinnie that he would come over and help him stack it into the garage.

Jimmie looked at me and said, "Did you order a lot of food." I told him I had an order coming tomorrow. He shook his head and said, "Excellent. Add to it and make sure you have enough of everything, because when we get a blizzard, the stores close, because the roads are impassable. If we lose electricity, you can put your stuff in the snow to keep it refrigerated or frozen. He asked Vinnie if he had enough propane and Vinnie said he would go get more tomorrow. Jimmie told him that he would be using the bbq if we lost electricity. He told me that Maria started making casseroles and baked them. Then they warm them on the bbq. He told us to round up all our warm blankets. He said, "We usually all hunker down in the living room where the fireplace is. I drag our mattress out there and the kids sleep in the playpen and we all stay in the warm room. Make sure you have plenty of water too. Add it to your list Nay, even if you think you have enough" We had all this leftover food and tomorrow I would start making some casseroles and prepping some stuff, just in case. I was getting a little nervous and asked Jimmie, "How much snow do you get in a blizzard. I am getting scared." Jimmie said, "We get FEET of snow, sometimes 4 -5 feet and with the wind, it drifts, so it looks like more. The wind is dangerous and it's almost like a winter hurricane. You will be ok, if you have wood, water, food, propane and blankets. And stay away from windows."

The kids had footie pajamas and I rounded up all the blankets I could. Vinnie dragged our mattress into the living room and we set everything up in there. He went and got more propane in our tank and bought an extra one, just in case. I added to my grocery list and got extra water, snacks for us and the kids, bread, eggs, milk, cereal, canned food, including corned beef hash, hotdogs, hamburgers, etc. We had a freezer full of chicken, steak and Pork tenderloins. I think we were all set. The load of wood was delivered and Vinnie opened the garage and had the guy dump it right inside. He moved the cars out, while it was being dumped. Once it was stacked, he would move them back in. Jimmie came as promised and they spent a few hours stacking it. I had no idea how much a cord of wood was and it was a lot. When the kids went in for a nap, I put the monitors on and went out in the garage. I got a pair of gloves on and pitched in. Vinnie and Jimmie just looked at me. I said, "What? I want to help too. This wood is a necessity and will keep us warm. The sooner we finish the better we will be."

They didn't say a word and just kept stacking. I asked if I could start a new stack in the corner and pointed to it and Vinnie said, "Yeah, that's good, go ahead." I found out that I was a good wood stacker and good at putting puzzles together. My stack looked better than theirs and they knew it and kept looking at each other. I stopped because I was tired and asked them if they wanted a cup of coffee. Vinnie said, "Yeah, sounds good, Make it a big Mug." Jimmie said a mug would be great. I brought them each a piece of cake too and a tray table and 2 folding chairs. They had about half hour more of work, but they were tired, so they sat there sipping the coffee and ate the cake. I looked at Jimmie and said, "Is there anything my mom and dad should do to prepare. I think my mom was getting scared yesterday when we were talking about it." He said, "You should tell them to come here and stay with you. Mary and Trevor too." He looked at Vinnie and said, "I will ask mom and dad if they want to stay with me and Maria. I just think they will be safer." Vinnie shook his head yes. I think he was nervous too. I called my mom and Mary and told them to pack up their clothes and blankets and anything else they needed and come to stay with us. "We have wood, propane, food and water, so you won't have to worry." They both accepted and my mom said, she was so relieved.

22

They came that afternoon and Jimmie helped Vinnie get the mattresses off the beds and downstairs in the living room. It's a good thing we had gigantic living room. We had a mattress on each side of the living room and the kids were in the middle. And the fireplace was on the other wall. That way no one was crowded. They moved the couches all the way to the wall and we moved some furniture around so it didn't look crowded. Mary and my mom made up their beds on the floor and Vinnie started the fire with Jimmie's help and Jimmie told him to keep it going and they both brought wood in and put it in the wood ring that Jimmie let us borrow. He told Vinnie to keep it roaring, even if it gets too hot in the house because he said we would appreciate it when it started snowing and the wind picked up. We set up a couple of battery operated stand fans to move the heat around the house. Jimmie said he went through two blizzards so far, so he knew what he was doing and Vinnie trusted him 100% and did everything he told him to do.

The kids were in their playpen and watching TV. Everyone was charging their phones, iPads and laptops. There were wires coming out of every outlet in the house, as I looked around, and I started laughing and took a few pictures. I was laughing now, but tomorrow I wouldn't be. Mom, Mary and me were in the kitchen preparing dinners and lunches and making breakfast sandwiches. My mom and Mary brought eggs and rolls and bacon and hamburgers and other things, so it wouldn't be all on us, which was nice. Vinnie and Jimmie went to Home Depot to get some Lanterns and batteries and came back with 10 of them. That way each person had their own lantern and we had one for the kitchen and bathrooms and a couple extra's. They bought a battery operated radio too, so we could get updates.

I knew we were ready for the storm with food and heat and everything, but <u>I was not</u> ready for this storm. I was scared to death. Vinnie heard it in my voice and he grabbed me and held me close. "We will be ok Nay. Jimmie got us all set up with everything we need. We will be fine hon."

We fried bacon and made shit loads of scrambled eggs and put cheese on them and put them in hard rolls and wrapped them up and made tuna salad and egg salad and I had bologna for the kids and we had chicken, turkey and ham deli meat. I had extra rolls in the freezer if we needed them. Mary made a chocolate cake with frosting and my mom made cinnamon rolls and I made some blueberry muffins and mixed up some pancake mix and made pancakes and waffles and put them in the freezer. I was making coffee in the Keurig and pouring it into our half gallon jugs. I made a gallon of coffee and put it in the fridge. The guys came in and couldn't believe all the food we had made. Jimmie started laughing and said, "I'm gonna call Maria and tell her I am staying here." I laughed and sent him home with some cake, muffins and cinnamon rolls and we got busy making more.

I saw Vinnie coming in with more wood for the wood ring and I pulled him aside. "Can you do me a favor?" He looked at me and said, "Sure hon, what's up?" I whispered in his ear. "*Can you go get my cardinal wind chimes and hang them in the garage for the winter?*"

He smiled at me and said, "Done." He put the wood in the ring and went out to get them and hung them on a hook in the garage. I saw Mary looking out the window and she smiled at me. "You don't have to tip toe around me. I am fine. I took my wind chimes in for the winter too." I told her that I didn't want her to get upset.

We all finished cooking and baking and we cleaned up and now it was shower time for me because I was exhausted. Vinnie got in with me and we got hot and heavy and figured it was a good time, since we had a shit load of house guests and they were watching the kids.

My mom and Mary had bathed the kids and had them in their PJ's by the time we got out, which was awesome and I thanked them for saving me from having to do it. Vinnie and I got their bottles ready and settled them down in their cribs to go to sleep. They had a full day of running around and spending time with their grandparents. They hit their pillows and they were out.

We all slept in the living room that night because our mattresses were already in there.

The weather channel said the snow was supposed to start during the night and the wind would pick up by morning. We all settled into our make shift beds and everyone fell asleep, except me. Well, I think I was the only one not sleeping. Vinnie looked like he was sleeping, but he turned his head and whispered, *"You ok Nay?"* I whispered back, *"Yeah, just nervous."* He put his arm around me and held me tight and whispered back, *"We will be ok. Stop worrying and go to sleep."* I finally fell asleep and when I woke up, it was 9:30. Holy Crap.

Everyone was up and moving around, but they were super quiet. The kids were up and dressed and eating breakfast and Vinnie had everything under control.

My mom was in the kitchen with Mary and they were making coffees in the Keurig. Oh God, I needed one of those… and before I finished my thought, Vinnie was kneeling in front of me with my cup of coffee. He sat on the mattress next to me and said, "You needed that sleep and there is nothing to do today, so just take it easy and rest. Did you see outside yet?" I stretched my neck to see if I could see out the window without getting up off the floor, but all I saw was the snow falling. It wasn't really windy yet. He said, "Plenty of time to see it. Pretty soon you won't have to stretch to see it because it's almost up to the window sill now." I looked at him shocked. "Really? Already?" He shook his head. "Come on, Come and see." He took my hand to help me off the floor and I bent over to get my coffee and walked to the window. "Holy Shit Vinnie. I have never seen this much snow in my whole life." He said, "I know, right? Me either."

Mary came in with Jamie and said, "I caught him drinking my coffee. Good thing it's decaf. In the playpen little one." She put him in and he sat down to play with his toys. She was shaking her head as she headed back to the kitchen. I started laughing and so did Vinnie. My mom came in with her coffee and stood right next to me at the window. "This is freaking amazing. I have never seen so much snow. I just hope it doesn't get bad." She patted me on the back and said, "Did you sleep good hon?" I told her I didn't get to sleep right away but when I did, I slept sound.

She walked back into the kitchen and her and Mary were sitting at the kitchen bar eating a cinnamon roll and having coffee. They were deep in conversation and Vinnie snapped a picture of the two of them. My dad and Trevor were sitting by the fireplace and Vinnie threw a couple more logs on to keep it going. Lily Bear was sitting with Papa Madden and going back and forth to Papa Trevor. They both adored her and would do anything for her and she knew it. She played the both of them like an instrument.

It started getting windy and I kept hearing creaking and squeaking coming from somewhere. I looked at Vinnie, "Did you hear that? What is it and where is it coming from?" I was getting scared. He listened, and he heard it too. He gathered my dad and Trevor and they listened and then everyone got quiet.

He texted his brother. "What do you think it could be Jimmie? Everyone is scared here, even me." His brother said, "Can you get outside and look at the roof?" Vinnie told him he would open the front door and see if he could get outside. Jimmie called him on the phone so he could hear what was going on. Vinnie opened the door and said there was no drift at the front door so he could step out on the porch. He stepped out and looked up at the roof. It was piled high with about 5 feet of snow from the wind drifting it. He snapped a picture and sent it to Jimmie.

Jimmie got the picture and he said, "Oh Crap, Vinnie, you guys have to get that off the roof ASAP. Do you have a leaf blower that you hold? Vinnie told him that we did. Vinnie ran out in the garage and got it with the longest extension cord he could find. They plugged it into the outside outlet and turned it on. It sent some of the snow flying, but the rest just stayed there. Vinnie was asking me if I heard the creaking anymore. I listened and didn't hear it. He kept the blower going and tried to get as much snow off the roof as possible. All it was, was a drift right over the living room and the last thing we need right now, was the roof collapsing on top of all of us. The rest of the roof was clear.   This is crazy, just friggin crazy.

The wind started picking up even more, and it was actually moving Vinnie. I leaned out the door and told him to unplug the blower and get in the house. "This wind is getting dangerous babe, get in here and let the wind move the rest of it." He brought it inside and put it back in the garage. We moved all our stuff out of the living room, and put it in the sitting room, and stayed in there, just in case.

I mean we wouldn't be able to stay there if the room collapsed, but at least no one would get hurt. Everyone pitched in and started dragging mattresses and Vinnie took the kids and they moved the playpen to the back of the house. We listened and didn't hear the creaking and squeaking anymore. The wind blew a branch off the tree in front and it hit the picture window in the living room and I thought I shit my pants. It didn't break, but it was so loud and everyone jumped.

Vinnie and my dad went out in the garage and they found a piece of plywood, or a piece of sheetrock that was a good size and they brought it in and put it against the window, just in case something else hit and broke the window. This was so if it broke, the glass wouldn't fly in. Vinnie told everyone to stay out of the living room for now. He stepped out on the front porch again to see if the snow was still there and it was gone. The wind blew it all away and our roof was clear.

He came in with snow in his hair and on his eyelashes and in his mustache and beard. "It's fucking cold out there. Holy Shit." I giggled when I saw him. I got a blanket and put it on his shoulders and rubbed him on his back and arms. I pushed him toward the fireplace and he sat down in front of it. He looked up at me and said, "The roof is clear, I think we are ok. I am gonna text Jimmie to let him know." I handed him his phone and he texted his brother to let him know we were ok and that everything was out of the living room. Jimmie texted back a smiley face and Vinnie asked how he was doing. He said he had the same problem for about a half hour, but the snow was clear. Jimmie called him. "Dude, when all this snow shit is over, I want you to have your roof checked and make sure it's sturdy." Vinnie said, "You don't have to tell me twice. This shit is scary."

Everyone had some lunch and we fed the kids and they were ready to take their naps, so we put them in the playpens and took the toys out. Jamie had a warm bottle of milk and Lily Bear had her Binky, we covered them with blankets and they settled down.

Everyone went somewhere in the house so they wouldn't have any distractions. Vinnie and I went up in the bedroom for 30 minutes and I think everyone else did the same. I peeked at them and they were asleep, so I spread the word and everyone came back to our gathering place.

I took out some brownies and we made a cup of coffee/tea and sat around quietly. The wind was getting even worse than it was this morning.

Vinnie turned on the TV and they were saying that the bad part of the storm didn't even hit yet. Of course, it was expected tonight. I think we already had 4 feet of snow and it was above the bottom of the picture window in the front of the house.

We heard something fall in the front yard and Vinnie peeked around the sheetrock to see what it was. It was the big tree in the center of the yard. Oh Thank God it didn't hit the house. I sat there and Thanked GOD. He said it fell sideways and it blocked the driveway. It shook the whole house when it hit the ground.

The weather channel had pictures of damage already and pictures of people stuck on the highway in their cars. How stupid can you be? You know there is a blizzard and you are on the highway? There were roads blocked, trees down on houses and they showed the whole mall closed. No stores were open anywhere.

We were close to Buffalo, NY and they always got it the worst, when we had snow. They always got buried, but I think we were a close second with this storm.

The kids slept for a couple hours and then they got up and had a snack. It was 3:00 p.m. and for some reason, I took out one of the chicken and rice casseroles and took a vote to see who wanted it for supper and everyone agreed. I put it in the oven on bake. My mom looked at me and said, "Nay, it's only 3:00 hon." I whispered to her that I had a feeling we were going to lose electricity soon and I wanted to have a hot meal. She shook her head. "Yeah, you are probably right, but Vinnie has the BBQ and blacktop in the garage right?" I shook my head, "Yes for when we lose it."

I was able to bake the whole casserole. It came out of the oven at 4:00 and I took paper plates and silverware out and told everyone to get it while it was hot. We usually didn't eat until 6 or so, and it was a little early, but I told everyone that we would probably lose electricity, so there would be no heating it up.

Everyone got up and got a plateful and we all sat down to eat. Vinnie and I got the kids plates ready and the lights started blinking.

He got my Dad and Trevor to help him with the lanterns and they brought them all into the dining room. He fed Jamie and I helped Lily Bear. She was pretty good by herself, so I was just assisting. While we were eating the lights blinked again and then we lost all electricity. Little Jamie started crying, because everyone made a scared sound when it went out.

Trevor put another log on the fire and my dad turned on the lanterns. My mom took Jamie out of the highchair and she consoled him while I consoled Lily Bear and told her we were going to have a night picnic. I finished feeding her in my lap and Vinnie finished feeding Jamie and everything calmed down.

Everyone finished eating and we were all carrying our lanterns around to see. All the paper plates went into the garbage and we rinsed the forks and put them in the dishwasher for now. Everyone took turns holding the kids so they wouldn't be scared. I was holding Jamie and I put their toys back in the playpens and we put them in and had a lantern lit right outside of the pens, so they could see and they were fine.

All of sudden, we heard loud Thunder and then more thunder. The snow was coming down so heavy that it looked like a sheet of white outside. I got scared and Vinnie hugged me and then he told everyone that it was called 'Thundersnow'. "It happens when there is heavy snow falling. It doesn't happen all the time and it's kind of rare, but it does happen, and if you look outside, it is coming down in buckets."

He put a couple more logs on the fire and got it roaring hot. He had a battery operated stand fan in the living room and had it on blowing directly into the sitting room to keep it warm where we were. My mom put cartoons on her iPad that she saved and the kids were watching so quiet. I was thankful for that because I don't think we had internet. Vinnie sent a text to Jimmie to see if everything was ok and then tried to call him and it didn't go through. I am sure Jimmie was trying to contact him too.

The snow continued to fall and we were getting about 8 inches an hour and now the snow came up past the picture window about 10 inches.

The wind wasn't getting any worse, and it stayed the same all day. It was about 50-55 mph and scary as hell. I could feel the temperature dropping in the house and Vinnie was keeping up with the fire. Trevor and my Dad helped him bring more wood in from the garage and they got it roaring again. He had the battery fan running to blow the heat toward us in the sitting room.

I told Vinnie that as long as the snow wasn't piling up on the roof, that we should all move back into the living room where it was hot and comfortable and he said, we should be ok doing that, so everyone dragged their mattresses back into the living room and we moved the kids back too. He put the fan in front of the fireplace and had it circulating back and forth to move the hot air around. I was so much warmer.

My mom was cold, so I gave her a fleece blanket and put it over her shoulders and gave her some fleece pajama bottoms to put over her stretch pants and a pair of my fleece slippers and socks. The smile on her face was priceless. I asked her if she was warmer and she smiled at me and said, "I am toasty. Thanks Hon."

Vinnie checked the kids and they were fine. We kept them in their footy pajamas with T-shirts and pants underneath, so they would be insulated. They both had slipper socks on underneath too.

Diaper changes were a pain in the butt because we had to take off the footy pajamas and then the pants and then the diaper and then put everything back on, but if it meant they were warm and comfy, it was worth it. Everyone kind of took turns helping out with it.

Vinnie put his coat on and went out in the garage to get the bbq and Blackstone near the garage door. He came in and asked if anyone wanted coffee or hot cocoa. I wanted hot cocoa and my mom and Mary wanted coffee. He warmed up the Blackstone and poured some coffee in a pot that I made the day before and he had a pan of milk for cocoa and had another small pan of water on the Blackstone. He put Jamie's bottle in the small pan of water to warm his milk, made my cocoa and poured coffee for my mom, Mary and himself. I went out to help him and brought out the metal serving tray and he balanced the cocoa and coffees on it.

I brought the bottle in for Jamie. My dad had him in his pj's for the night and changed him and offered to give him his bottle. I thanked him, but I wanted him in the playpen to drink the bottle so he could go to sleep.

We put both kids down for the night and we went in the sitting room, while they dozed off and then we went back to the living room.

Everyone was sipping coffee or cocoa and sitting on their mattress playing on their iPads or their phones. My dad had a solar charger and he had put it in the front window during the day and it charged right up with the light coming in and he used it to charge up his phone and iPad. Vinnie got up and brought in a tray of cookies that we made. Everyone's face lit up, because we were all bored to death. What do you do when you are bored to death? You eat cookies in the dark with your family. According to my phone, if it was correct, we had one more day of snow.

Vinnie was nervous about his brother not answering. He checked his phone and it said we were connected to the internet, so he sent another text to his brother. A couple minutes went by and his phone rang. It was Jimmie.

Everyone was ok and he told Vinnie that they didn't have internet for a while but it was back and he said it was going in and out intermittently. Vinnie was so relieved and they talked for a few minutes and then hung up. Now he was smiling and that made me happy.

It was a long boring night, just sitting there on the mattresses, on the floor, playing games on our iPads. We were occasionally talking to one another, but mostly we were all quiet. I got tired of sitting up, so I laid down, and Vinnie said, in 2 minutes I was out like a light and he covered me up and I slept all night.

He got up and loaded up the fireplace with wood around 2:00 a.m. to keep it going. He told everyone that if they got up during the night, to add a log or two so it wouldn't go out. My dad got up at 4:00 a.m. and he put a couple logs on and my mom got up at 6:00 to pee, so she put a couple on and then Trevor got up at 8:00 and he put a couple logs on, so that worked out good.

It was nice and toasty when I woke up at 8:30 and the kids were just getting up. They were really good sleepers and always have been.

They took after their mommy in that respect. Lily Bear was a hard one to get up, even after she woke up. She always wanted to just stay there and veg out. I guess she was warm and comfortable. Yup, she took after me. I could stay in bed all day. Jamie took after Daddy though. Once he was awake, he got right up and was raring to go. Vinnie warmed up the Blackstone and put the breakfast sandwiches on it and left them wrapped in the tinfoil. He gave the kids some milk and he made them some scrambled eggs and even some toast. The Blackstone was a lifesaver.

I checked the freezer and I think it was too warm in there, so me and Vinnie emptied it into a cooler and put the cooler on the deck and filled it with snow to save what we had. We cooked the hamburgers and hotdogs and we made 2 pork tenderloins and we had frozen vegetables that started to defrost, so we cooked them up too and we had lunch and dinner cooked. The rest was in the cooler and was fine. We just kept adding snow to make sure it stayed frozen.

The snow continued all day and started tapering off and so did the wind. I laid in bed with the kids and Vinnie and I were playing with them. It's hard to keep them busy in the dark. I mean we had the lanterns on and we already had to change all the batteries once, but it's not the same as when the sun is out. They were a little cranky and I didn't know what to do with them. Vinnie went to get their ride on's and we put a gate in front of the stairs, so they wouldn't go down. That took care of an hour during the morning and then it was lunch time and we put them in their highchairs. They each had an egg salad sandwich and 2 peanut butter crackers and milk and they were full. It was nap time, so we each took one and changed them and down they went. They were tired after riding their cars around, so it didn't take long.

Finally, the snow stopped around 3:00 p.m. It was still windy, but not like it was during the storm. Vinnie opened the front door and it was a wall of snow about 4 feet high and some fell into the house. He said, "Wooaahhh. Holy Shit. Babe, get the shovel please?" I ran to get it and he started shoveling the snow onto the front porch. He took a couple pictures before he did and sent it to his brother.

I couldn't believe how high it was. We were definitely snowed in. Trevor and my dad were loading up the wood ring for the day and everyone was doing some chores. Mary was cleaning the downstairs bathroom and my mom was doing the upstairs one. I swept up the wood chips and stuff in front of the fireplace and then went into the kitchen and washed a few things that were in the sink and put them on the drying mat. I swept up the kitchen and dining room floor and got the crumbs cleaned up. I had to keep a little busy today because I was going crazy being cooped up like this, especially all in one room. I just wanted to lay in bed and do nothing. I was fucking bored stiff.

When everyone was done, the kids were playing nice in their playpen and Vinnie brought out Monopoly and asked who wanted to play. Everyone was dying to do something, so they all agreed. We sat at the dining room table and Vinnie and my Dad pulled the playpen in there with us so we could keep an eye on the little buggers.

They loaded up the fireplace and we played the game all afternoon until dinner time. Vinnie went out to warm up all the food we made earlier and we all ate dinner. We ate the pork tenderloins and the veggies and we made some success rice on the Blackstone. We put the hamburgers in buns and wrapped them up earlier, along with the hotdogs and put them in a Ziploc bag and they went into the cooler with snow on top. That would be lunch or dinner for tomorrow.

We lived like this for another 2 days and then we got electricity back. The sun was out and the snow was melting and the plows were doing the roads and highways. The stores were still not open, but we had plenty of food and snacks and desserts. Everyone put on their coats, boots and scarfs and started shoveling the driveway and sidewalks. We weren't in any hurry. We took the kids out and Vinnie took them sledding down the driveway a few times before we shoveled and they had so much fun.

Mary was watching them because we didn't want her to shovel. They couldn't go very far, because the snow was higher than them.

After about a half hour, she took them in the house to get warm and Trevor went inside to help with them. We were out for another 1/2 hour and then we came in. We weren't done, but we were frozen. Trevor had the fire roaring and had shots of Blackberry brandy waiting for all of us. It was getting dark already and it was only 4:30 p.m. I put another casserole in the oven for dinner and I made some dinner rolls. Vinnie opened a bottle of wine and we all had some at dinner. The guys put all the mattresses back upstairs on the beds and we cleaned up the living room.

The kids went down for the night in their cribs in their own bedrooms and Vinnie and I headed up to take a shower and… Yes, we did. We got in our PJ's and headed back downstairs and I decided I was going to finish the wine. Vinnie helped me and we were a little tipsy, but not really drunk. I was toasty and flushed and felt really good.

We went upstairs to our bedroom and I fell asleep about 2 hours later and slept all night. Vinnie still kept the fire going and whoever got up during the night put logs on. We had our heat on, but we wanted to keep it warm. We had the doors closed at night because we weren't down there to keep an eye on it.

We went out the next day to finish shoveling the driveway and the roads were all clear, so our guests packed up and left that day and thanked us for putting them up and keeping them safe. I think my mom was a little sad when she was leaving. She enjoyed being with the kids during the day. I told her she could come over whenever she wanted and didn't need an invitation. "You live so close now so there is no excuse. Just come over when you want to."

Everyone cleaned up before they left and everything was put back where it was. All the beds were made with clean sheets and the living room furniture was all put back. They even vacuumed every room. I had nothing to do except laundry. We put everything back in the freezer and Vinnie put the cooler back in the garage.

We kept the bbq and Blackstone in the garage near the door. We weren't going anywhere very soon.

We both started in on the laundry. We did sheets first because there were a lot of them. The clothes were minimal because we all stayed in PJ's for a couple of days. The kids had the most clothes because we dressed them everyday and put footie pjs on over the top.

Crowley and Crowley, M.D.'s were open with minimal hours and they told Vinnie to stay home for the rest of this week. He didn't complain about it and was happy to be here with me and the kids and I was happy he was home with me.

It was Monday, so we had the rest of the week to spend together. The stores started to open up so we made a list and did an Instacart order for just a few things. We ordered Sushi for supper one night and we had leftovers for the kids. We enjoyed each other every single night in bed and in the shower and it was like the old days, before the kids.

23

***

It was May and getting warmer now and I was taking the kids out for some fresh air and we would walk up and down the driveway and the sidewalks and they loved it. I let them play with a ball in the front yard because it was fenced in and they were safe out there. I took there cars outside and they went up and down the sidewalk with them. One day, LilyBear stopped in her tracks, while riding her bike and said, "Mommy, I hear a kitty meowing." I grabbed Jamie and walked over and listened and sure enough I heard it too. It sounded like babies crying. Lily got off her car and peeked into a front bush. Something moved and scared the crap out of her and she jumped back and started crying.

I grabbed her and put her and Jamie up on the front porch and told them to stay put. I peeked into the bush and sure enough, there were 2 baby kittens. I looked to see if there were anymore and even checked the other bushes along the front of the house and nothing, No mommy around and no other siblings. These babies had to be about 4 weeks old. I picked them up, one in each hand and showed the kids. "Look what mommy found. Two baby kitties and no mommy. Lily's little heart melted when she actually saw what moved. "Mommy, can we keep them?" I looked at her and said, "Can you be a good mommy for them?" She shook her head yes, while she was smiling from ear to ear. I said, "Well, I suppose we can keep them, but we need to get some baby bottles and kitten milk and some beds and blankets to take care of them, and they need a bath." Lily started jumping up and down.

I told both of them that they had to be very gentle with them because they were tiny babies and if you hurt them, they will die. They both looked at me very serious and they knew what that meant because of cartoons that they watched. I carried the kittens in the house and held the door and the kids followed me in. I went into the bathroom and put both kittens in the sink.

I told Lily to watch them and not let them out of the sink. I went to get some Dawn dish liquid and put a couple towels in the dryer. I filled the other sink with warm water and took one kitten at a time and bathed them with Dawn. I thought they would have been covered in fleas, but there weren't any. I guess because it was early in the season. I wrapped the bathed kitten in the warm towel and handed it to Lily. "Be careful honey. They are very delicate. Ok?" She took the kitten and sat on her foot stool and Jamie was petting it. I washed the other and put that one in the other warm towel. I said, "Ok guys, let's dry them really good ok?" I took out the hair dryer and put it on low and I took an old baby brush out of the drawer and I brushed them and dried each one.

They were both purring so loud. I texted a picture to Vinnie and said, "You said I could get kittens, but no dog. Lily found them in the bushes out front and they are about 4 weeks old. We need to go do some shopping. I need kitten milk and bottles and stuff. You ok with this?"

He texted me right back. "They are so adorable. Yes, I am more than ok with it. I am coming home early and we will go pet shopping." He was home 15 minutes later. I had the kittens wrapped up in a blanket and they were so hungry and crying. We got the kids ready, I grabbed the kittens and we were off the Pet Smart. I saw Vinnie smiling while Lily told him the story about finding the kittens.

We brought the kittens into the store and all the girls were oohing and ahhing over them and they showed us where to find the milk and bottles and beds and they were actually following us around with a basket. We got 6 bottles because the girls said they sometimes bite the tops. We got a few boxes of kitten milk. We bought 2 kitten beds, even though they would probably sleep together in one.

We bought them a brush and some dry and wet kitten food and we got them an enclosed playpen. We got a couple of litter boxes and litter. Food and water dishes and a water fountain. The girls gave us a few business cards to vets in the area and told us that we should have them checked out because it looked like the mother abandoned them and they sometimes do that if they think there is

something wrong with them. I took cards for
the four closest vets in the area.

The kids were all excited and I think Vinnie was
too. We all went home and I held the kittens in
the car, and they were so hungry. I couldn't
wait to get home and feed them. We told the
kids that we would feed them first and they
could watch how to do it, and then they could
feed them next. Those kittens sucked that
milk down so fast and I felt so bad for them.

Vinnie said, "You guys want to name your new
kittens? They have to be good names though.
You think about it for a while and then we will
all take votes ok?" They shook their heads
and they were all excited. Both kittens were
tabbies with black down the middle of their
backs and their underbellies were an Amber

color and they had little gray and black stripes
down their sides and on their tail. They had
beautiful markings. They had the 'M' on their
forehead. They really were beautiful little
babies and I was in love with both of them
already.

I told Vinnie that I wanted to name one of the
them and he asked me what the name was
and I told him Sushi. He loved it and he told

the kids that they only had to find a name for one cat because mommy wanted to pick a name and he told them that one of them was Sushi. One of the kittens had a solid Black tip on his/her tail and that one would be Sushi and he showed them. They loved the name I picked and they weren't upset like I thought they would be.

Sushi could be a boy or a girl and we needed another name like that because we didn't know if they were boys or girls. Vinnie explained to the kids, or tried to, that the name had to be for a girl or a boy. He told them if they couldn't think of one, then he would name the cat. I whispered to him. *"You have a name, don't you?"* He laughed and whispered back, *"Yup, Mochi"*. I said, "OMG, I love that name". The kids heard me and they wanted to know, so he told the kids and they loved it. So those were the names.

Sushi and Mochi were our new family members. The kids were getting so excited because they were going to feed them next. We set them up in their upholstered chairs (that Gramma Mary bought them) and we each handed them a kitten and a bottle and they did great. They were so gentle with them.

Vinnie explained that they were going to get bigger and when they did, we still had to treat them gently and with love and kisses. They did a good job feeding them and they kissed them and petted them and then I picked them up and put them together in one of the beds, inside the playpen and covered them with a blanket. The kids sat on each side of the playpen, just watching them for almost an hour. They were in love with them. Vinnie took a picture of them feeding them and then another one of them sitting on each side of the playpen watching them and sent them to everyone with a text that said, "Meet our 2 new additions to the family, Sushi and Mochi. Lily found them in the bush outside the front door."

For the time being, the litter boxes were in the living room, along with the beds and food and water dishes. They would stay there while they were little. I put a blanket down in the corner behind our couch and put the litter box on top of it and then a few feet away was their food and water and then their beds. So they were all along the front wall of the living room, but behind the couch. But at night, a litter box, water and one bed went inside the playpen and they were zipped up, to keep them safe from getting into anything.

The texts started coming back to Vinnie about the kittens. Everyone was so excited to come and see them and Vinnie said to give them a few days to get acclimated and we needed to take them to the vet first.

The next morning I called the vet that was down the street, across from where Vinnie worked and told them my story and they asked if I was available to bring them both in now because they had a cancellation. I told them I would be there in 10 minutes. I got the kids' shoes on and a light jacket and out we went. I had the kids hold one kitten each while I was driving and realized that we needed a pet carrier at that moment. We took them in for an examination and they were very healthy considering they were feral kittens. I told the vet that I bathed them and told them what we were feeding them.

I asked him some questions about when we should start feeding dry food and he told me in about a week but to keep giving them the milk, because they needed that to grow. I told him that they were using the litter box and he was shocked because he said that feral cats don't usually do that right away.

He gave them the dewormer and said they were too young for a lot of the shots, so we made another appointment to bring them back in a month when they were 8 weeks old. We left the vet and headed toward Pet Smart and I bought a pet carrier, just big enough for the 2 of them. Later on, I would have to buy another one when they got bigger, but this one was good for now.

The kittens were the main attraction these days, for everyone. The kids were fascinated by them and they were so good with them. They were gentle and loving with both of them. I made sure I clipped their nails once a week, to keep them short. I didn't want the kids to get scratched and I warned them about the nails.

My mom and dad came over and Lily Bear was the spokes person and told all the stories starting with finding them in the bush, their bath and feeding them bottles like a baby. She remembered every detail and told it all. It's a good thing I don't have any secrets. LOL.

The same thing happened when Gramma and Papa Greco came to see them and Jamie got in on the story telling this time. Lily let him tell a couple of stories and then took over. I never saw either of them talk so much. Vinnie said that the kittens were the best thing that could have happened for the kids and I agreed. He said, "It teaches them responsibility, how to care for an animal and be kind and how to love another living creature." Of course, when Mary and Trevor came, they both told the stories all over again and Lily was teaching Gramma Mary how to hold Sushi and Papa Trevor how to hold Mochi. "No, Like this Papa, not like that." He smiled at her and said, "Thank you for teaching me Lily, because Papa never had a kitten." She looked at him shocked, "God didn't send you a kitten Papa?" Trevor had tears in his eyes and he quickly wiped them away. He looked at me and I said, "Cartoons papa. They both learned that from Cartoons." He shook his head. He told Lily that God gave him a little girl, but not a kitten. She didn't ask him any questions and I was happy about that. I told him later that we also did prayers before bed because they learned that too. He said, "Nothing wrong with that at all. Good Job Nay." I told him that I told them all about my best friend and now she is in heaven and she comes to visit in the window and she is a red cardinal. He said, "You told them about her?" I hugged him and said, "Of course I did. Rain was my best friend. We may have had a fight, but she was still my best friend." I paused and told him that I showed them pictures of her when we were little and then when we were older. Lily understood a little better than Jamie did because she was older.

She was a smart little girl and picked everything up so fast. She was smart like her Daddy. Vinnie sat with her and taught her how to write her ABC's and how to write her numbers 1-10 and she did really good. She knew how to write her name too.

She was 4 now and Kindergarten was on the horizon. I couldn't believe how fast time went by. Jamie was losing his baby face and he was 3. Vinnie was also teaching him his ABC's and his numbers, but just to say them for now. Writing would come once he learned how to say them. He was also a smart cookie and picked everything up quick too. He was momma's boy for now. It changes monthly and that is ok with me.

They were both attached to me and that was because they were with me all day. I took them outside to play during the day, when it was warm and sunny. Lily Bear got a tricycle from her Daddy and he was teaching her how to ride it. It took her all of 2 hours and she was zooming around and turning it and having so much fun with it. Jamie was watching her and when she got off it, he got on and just started riding it and we all thought it was hysterical. Daddy better go by another one quick. He went the next day and got Jamie his own tricycle and the both of them had a blast with them.

Sushi and Mochi were getting big fast and they were off the bottles and eating wet and dry food on their own. They went back to the vet and got their shots and they were all up to date. The vet said they were healthy. Sushi was a boy and Mochi was a girl. We made appointments for them to be fixed in four months.

The kids always held the kittens in their laps while they were watching TV and they petted them and talked to them sweetly. Both kittens were very affectionate with the kids and they were careful with them as well. I never once saw any claws come out and they rubbed their faces on them and showed them affection.

Uncle Jimmie came with Maria, Kyle and baby Ruthie to see the kittens and Lily Bear and Jamie were so happy to see them. Lily Bear stayed true to character and told the stories about the kittens and she remembered it all from the day we found them. Maria was listening intently and she smiled at me during the stories.

She told me later that she couldn't believe how good she told the stories. Lily Bear sat in Uncle Jimmie's lap and asked him if God sent him kitties yet and he answered her quickly

and said, "Not yet honey, but we asked him
and I think he will bring some very soon.
When he sends them, I will invite you to come
and see them ok?" She was absolutely
delighted with his answer and said, "Ok, I will
help you with them. You have to be gentle and
kiss them all the time and you have to love
them Uncle Jimmie, lots and lots." He hugged
her and said, "I know and I will do that and you
can help me when they come." Kyle was 7,
almost 8 years old and he was smirking at her.
His father gave him a look and he stopped. He
hugged his cousin and said, "I will love them
too Lily."

Kyle was a good kid, but he was learning
certain things from other kids in school, and
Jimmie was nipping that in the bud. All he had
to do was look at him in a certain way and
Kyle knew the shit was gonna hit the fan. I
knew our day was coming with that, but I was
hoping that Lily Bear wouldn't learn to many
bad things. We taught her right from wrong
and how to believe in herself and do what is
right and not to listen to other kids. We told
her that she should listen to adults that are in
charge. She listened to us when we talked to
her and we heard her telling Jamie what we
told her, so I was keeping my fingers crossed.

A couple weeks later, Uncle Jimmie called Vinnie and asked to speak with Lily Bear. She took the phone from her Daddy and said, "Who is this please?" Now I was snickering under MY breath. This kid was something else. Vinnie put the phone on speaker and put it on the counter in the kitchen. "This is Uncle Jimmy, Lily Bear. I just called to let you know that God brought me two kittens and I think I need some help to take care of them. Can you show me what to do?" She had the biggest smile on her face and said, "Yes, Uncle Jimmie, I will help you, but Daddy has to bring me over." She looked up at her father and said, "Daddy can you bring me over Uncle Jimmie's house? He needs help with his kitties." Vinnie shook his head and said, "Yes, I think I can do that."

I had this feeling of something come over me and I started tearing up. I was proud, I was happy, and I think I was sad, because she was growing up. She looked at me and said, "Mommy, don't cry, you can come with us." I bent down and said, "Oh ok, yes, I would love to come with you. Can I help you with the kittens?" She kissed me on the cheek and said, "Yup, I will need some help too." I had to go in the other room and compose myself. Jamie was in the kitchen with them, just listening and I heard him ask if he could help too. Lily took his hand and said, "Yes, you can help too Jame." She was the boss and she was taking charge of the whole thing.

We had just finished lunch, so I cleaned up and we all went to see Uncle Jimmie's kittens. They were absolutely the cutest little things. They were Bengal Kittens, so they looked totally different from what we had. Jimmie bought them and told Vinnie that he always wanted a Bengal Kitten and after seeing ours, he decided he would get two. Lily looked at them and said, "They are a different color with big spots. What is wrong with them?" I guess she thought that all kittens looked the same.

Uncle Jimmy googled cats and sat her on his lap and made her look at all the different cats and then she understood. The kittens were 7 1/2 weeks old and didn't need a bottle, but he told her that he wanted to know how to hold them and pet them and she went right to work and showed him everything. This kid was going to be a vet.

She picked them up so gently and said, "You have to hold their feet, so they don't stretch." I was giggling under my breath. She taught Uncle Jimmie everything I taught her and she even showed him how to kiss them. "You can hug them, but not to tight because you will hurt them. If you hurt them, they will die, and God will not be happy with you." Jimmie looked at me and I shrugged my shoulders. I whispered, *"I don't know where she got that from. That is not something I told her."* Jimmie said, "Lily, who told you that?" She looked him straight in the face and said, "God gave you the kittens as a gift and if you don't take care of them, he will be upset. No one told me that." Vinnie was stunned and I think we all were.

Vinnie leaned into me and said, "What are they watching on TV? I mean it's nothing bad at all, but I didn't know they teach this on TV." This little girl was only 4 years old and I never ever saw a 4 year old talk like this. She was above and beyond for her age. She was so serious while she told this story about God being upset.

Jamie looked at me and said, "Mommy, if you give me a present and I step on it. You would be upset. Right?" I looked at Vinnie and Jimmy and started to cry. This kid was 3 years old. Where the hell were these kids learning this? Whatever program it was, was awesome. It was teaching them life lessons and what other people would feel like, if you did something bad to them.

I decided to sit with them while they were watching this program. They explained to the kids that animals were Gods gift to people to take care of. They were teaching them that bullying was a bad thing and to talk nice to people. The program was excellent and I loved it. At first, I thought it was a Christian Program, but it wasn't. It was teaching them everything they needed to go out in the world and be good people.

24

***

Vinnie and I took Lily to get registered for Kindergarten and Papa Greco babysat for Jamie. It was a very interesting day and Lily made it that way. She was so grown up for almost 5 years old and she let it be known to the teacher that she would help her teach the kids. Me and Vinnie looked at each other and giggled under our breath. We looked at the teacher and she was smiling and said, "Well, I can use all the help I can get. Thank you Lily. Maybe you can help with the alphabet? Do you know it?" Lily started reciting it and then said, "I can write it. Wanna see?" Mrs. Norton said, "Not today, but I will want to see when you start school ok?" She told Lily to go play with the toys on the other side of the room and she ran over. Mrs. Norton looked at us and we all just laughed. "She is a little spitfire huh?" We shook our heads and we told her that she catches on quick and she is very smart. She said, "Do you mind if I ask what you both do for a living?" Vinnie said, "We are both Physician Assistants, but my wife stays home right now with the kids." She raised her eyebrows and said, "She is a very, very smart child and now I know why. She probably <u>will</u> help me teach the class." She laughed and said, "Do you home school? Vinnie smiled and said, "Yes, we both do, with both of our children. You will probably have Jamie next year. He is Lily's Irish twin and they both have the same birthdays." We went back and forth with her asking her questions and she asking us. She was a very friendly person and we were going to get along great. We told her about the TV program that they both watch and how impressed we were with it.

The registration was over and we called Lily back over. She ran back and grabbed her Daddy and jumped up on him. Mrs Norton said, "Well, Lily, I can't wait to see you in September when school starts. Be a good girl ok?" She said, "I will Mrs. Norton. I will see you in September." The teacher was impressed that she remembered her name. Mrs. Norton asked where her brother was and she said, "He is with Papa Greco right now. Did you know that I have 3 papa's?" Mrs Norton said, "3 papas, wow, you are one lucky little girl. You must be very special to have 3 of them." She smiled at the teacher and said, "Yes, I am lucky. I have Papa Greco, Papa Madden and Papa Trevor and I have 3 Grandma's too. I have Gramma Greco, Gramma Madden and Gramma Mary, so I am super special."

Me and Vinnie were laughing and looking at each other. Mrs. Norton said, "How come you have 3?" She said, "Well, Papa Greco is my Daddy's father and Papa Madden is my Mommy's father, but Papa Trevor is my mommy's best friends' father and her best friend is in heaven and she visits us in the window. She is a pretty red bird. So I call him my papa." I started crying. She _really_ did understand. She did. Holy Shit. Vinnie wiped his eyes too. My little girl was unbelievable. Mrs. Norton said, "Well, that is an incredible story. What is your mommy's best friends name?" Lily said, "Her name is Lorraine and that is my middle name, but my mommy called her Rain." I stood up in shock. How did she know this? I never told her any of this. Vinnie stood up too. I picked her up and said, "Lily, who told you this honey? How do you know this?" She calmly said, "Grammy Mary". I sighed with relief. "Oh ok". I put her down and she ran to the toys. Mrs. Norton said, "You look like you saw a ghost." I told her that I never said anything to her about her name or what I called her or that she had her middle name. I told her about the bird and I didn't think she understood it, but she did. I told her I didn't know that Rain's mother explained it to her. I said, "Wow, sorry about all this. I just had no idea she knew about it." She smiled and said, "Well, it's all out in the open now."

We all laughed a nervous laugh. We took her home and we were quiet in the car because I didn't want to talk about it in front of her. I asked her if she liked Mrs. Norton and she said she did. We just asked her some questions about going to school and then we were home.

She ran off to play with Jamie and we had a conversation with Vinnie's dad about what happened at the Registration. Vinnie asked his dad, if she ever said anything to him and asked him if he knew that she knew. He shook his head no and had no idea that she knew about Rain. He said, "Maybe you should have a talk with Mary and Trevor about it?" I told him that I didn't care that she knew, but I was upset that they told her and didn't tell me that they told her, if that makes sense.

Lily was in the playroom with Jamie and she was telling him all about her new teacher and all the toys that were in the room. "I am going to help Mrs. Norton teach the class and I am going to write the alphabet for her on my first day." Jamie was fascinated with her stories and he wanted to know if he could go with her and she told him that he couldn't go yet because he wasn't old enough. He got upset and came running out to us and he started crying and saying that he wanted to go to school with Lily. Vinnie picked him up and consoled him and told him that he was going to go to school next year and he calmed down. The first day was not going to be fun for me, Vinnie or Jamie.

25

***

It's been such a long time since Vinnie and I have gone out together, ALONE. We haven't even been out to dinner in forever, and I told him one night when we were laying in bed. He looked at me and said, "Yeah, That is what's missing. I miss our date nights and we need to have them again. Let's go to The Water's Edge this Saturday night and have a nice dinner and then we can go play some mini golf or something. What do you think?" I hugged him and said, "It's a date. I Love you, Vinnie and I feel like we are growing apart. All you do is work and all I do is take care of the kids. We don't do anything fun for ourselves anymore." He hugged me tight. "The last thing I want is for us to grow apart. I love you with all my heart and soul and I will never let that happen."

The next day, he asked his parents to babysit on Saturday night and they were so excited to do it. He told them that from now on, they would be taking turns babysitting with my parents so we could go out together and do things on Saturday nights. They agreed. I texted my mom and did the same thing and they agreed and said they were available for next Saturday night. Yay, I was getting my Vinnie back. I loved date nights with him and I missed them so much. I missed my Vinnie, the Vinnie I met so long ago when I got punched. I don't miss the punching part, but I miss the part where he said, "You caught my eye" and all the parts after that, where he promised he would love me and protect me and make me happy for the rest of my life. I mean, he still is keeping his promise, but we need the intimacy, privacy, fun and dating that we had before the kids. I really needed it and I think he did too.

Saturday night came and Gramma and Papa Greco showed up to babysit. The kids were already fed, bathed and in their PJ's. They just had to be put to bed. Our reservations were at 7 and it was 6:15. Bedtime for the kiddos was 8:00 p.m. We both were dressed up. Vinnie wore dress pants and a dress shirt and I wore a nice black dress with flats.

Lily and Jamie fed their kitties some dry food and they were watching TV with them in their laps. We kissed them and told them to be good for Grammy and Papa.

We got in the car and headed out on our date to The Water's Edge. I looked at Vinnie and he was smiling. He said, "We are on a date babe. A real date." I laughed and said, "It's been a long time." He made the reservations because at night they were pretty busy. We had a corner table that was very romantic and they had candles lit at each table. The place looked totally different from when we used to come in the afternoon.

The last time we came here, was my last appointment with Dr. Nussear, just before Jamie was born 4 years ago. Vinnie pulled my chair out and I sat down and he sat next to me. We looked at the menu and I already knew what I wanted. I ordered a Water's Edge Punch, which was coconut rum, orange juice, pineapple juice, grenadine and a splash of soda. These things were outrageously delicious. I wanted their Fried Calamari and their Lobster Ravioli. Vinnie got their crab cake and their Lobster Roll with French Fries.

We chowed down and talked while eating and we were having such a good time.

We were on our main course, when we heard a commotion in the front of the restaurant and someone was yelling for help. "IS THERE A DOCTOR IN THE HOUSE? HELP, PLEASE HELP OMG". Vinnie and I got up and ran to the front of the restaurant and there was a man sitting at the table and he was choking and his wife was hysterical and people were just standing around looking at him. Vinnie picked him up from behind and did the Heimlich and out popped a piece of Filet Mignon. The woman was crying hysterically and the man was so thankful that Vinnie saved his life. They tried to give him money, but Vinnie told him it wasn't necessary and we walked back to our table to finish dinner. He started laughing a little when we sat down and said, "There is never a dull moment for us." I chuckled a little and said, "You saved someone's life Vinnie. You should be proud." He looked at me and said, "Yes, I am, but this was our date." I touched his hand and said, "It hasn't changed anything about our date. We are still on a date and I am so proud of you."

We finished eating our main course and he said, "I am full, but I am going to order dessert. I wanna try that Limoncello Cake. It's a yellow cake, soaked with Limoncello syrup and layered with lemon cream. How bout you?" My eyes lit up and I said, "I am in for that. It sounds yummy." The waiter came back and he ordered 2 of them and coffee to go with it. While we were waiting for it, the man he saved, came to our table with his wife to thank Vinnie again for saving his life and they left. I said, "That was nice of him, seeing as he already thanked you."

We ate our dessert and sipped our coffee and we were talking about Lily Bear and her registration day. I said, "She really is so smart Vinnie and she doesn't let on that she knows so much. She is so much like you. I see you in her every single day. Certain things that you do, she does. Even Jamie does things that you do. The way you swing your arm when you walk. Little things like that. Even facial expressions that you have. They both have them." I smiled at him and he said, "I see you in both of them too, a lot of you."

We finished our dinner and he asked me if I wanted to go play some mini golf or go to a movie. I picked a movie because I wanted to snuggle with him. We looked at some trailers to see what was out there because it has been ions since we went to a movie.

We picked one and then Vinnie waved the waiter over for the check. He took out his wallet and pulled out his credit card and the waiter came over with the black book and put it on the table and left. He opened it and the check had already been paid and the waiter was already tipped. It said $-0-. Thank you again. The man that he saved paid for our bill and even tipped the waiter $50. I got tears in my eyes and Vinnie was a little emotional too. "Wow, that was really nice of him." He got up and nodded to the waiter and handed him another $20. He told him that we wanted a standing reservation for 'our' table every Saturday night at 7:00 p.m. and asked him to write us in. The waiter smiled and said, "Yes sir. I will. Thank you."

Vinnie took my hand and we walked out of the restaurant and he held tight. He turned to me in the parking lot and kissed me with an open mouth and I felt things I haven't felt in a long time. He turned me on and it's been a long time since that happened. We were in a rut, we just did it because it was a habit. But tonight was going to be a different story. It wasn't going to happen because it was a habit. We made out in the car for a long time and the movie wasn't starting for a while. We may not even make the movie. OMG. He was fucking amazing and I felt like I was 23 again.

We did not make the movie…And I did not miss it at all. We ended up in a hotel and he texted his dad to let them know we were spending the night out. His father texted back, "🤣 😂. Ok, have fun. We will stay in the spare room."

We had such a good time that night. We never stayed in a hotel overnight, even when we were dating, except when we were on vacation. We chased each other and played with each other and had sex, over and over and we enjoyed each other almost the whole night. We knew the next day was gonna be hard with the kids, but we didn't care. We ordered breakfast in our room and had French toast and scrambled eggs and bacon and coffee. We loved each other so much and he said, "You still catch my eye babe and you always will. I love the fuck out of you." We showered and got dressed up in the clothes we came in and went home. The kids were up and dressed and they already ate breakfast. His father was snickering at us when we walked in and I looked at him, laughed and said, "Shut up" and I walked by him and he laughed at me.

His mom was just smiling and didn't say a word. Vinnie and I picked up the kids and kissed them. His mom said, "You guys look tired. Do you want us to stay?" I smiled at her and said, "Oh no, we are fine. Thank you for staying overnight. We needed a mini-vacation." She said, "Been there done that. We are here when you want to do it again. Everyone should do it." I smiled at her and pulled her in for a hug. "Thank you so much."

Vinnie and I got changed into sweats and settled in to watch TV with the kids. It was raining, so we couldn't take them outside, so it was just a lazy day.

We all had a sandwich and chips for lunch and I heated up some Chickarina soup with meatballs. It was comfort food because it was damp and cool outside and a little inside. Vinnie actually turned the heat up a little to make it go on and take the chill out of the house and then turned it back down. The kids loved that soup and I made sure I had plenty of it in the house. I usually made homemade Italian wedding soup in the winter and I put meatballs, egg noodles and spinach in it. I make huge pots of it and then I freeze it for a quick meal or lunch.

The kids went to play in the playroom in the afternoon and they were working on a jigsaw puzzle that Papa Greco bought them. He built them a big desk to make it on. The puzzle was a hard one and it was made for kids 10-12, but they were doing good with it.

Vinnie and I just vegged on the couch together, laying next to each other. I think I dozed off for a bit and I woke up startled. "Vinnie?" He touched me and said, "Right here babe." I said, "Oh God, I fell asleep and thought I left the kids alone. That scared the crap out of me."

He said, "I am awake and you did not leave them alone."

We both got up to check on them and they were still working on the puzzle and the cats were in the room with them talking up a storm and they were throwing balls for them to chase. Vinnie said, "How's it going guys? Did you find any pieces? Do you want some help?" Lily spoke up and said, "Yeah Dad, we found a couple pieces, but you can help if you want to." I came in and Lily said, "You wanna help mommy?" I smiled and said, "Sure, let's work on this together. It looks hard."

Vinnie and I pulled up a little chair and we all sat around the puzzle board looking for pieces." It was getting towards dinner time and Vinnie said, "Who wants burgers and fries?" Their faces lit up and they both wanted it, so he door dashed dinner and I was so thankful for that. We had a little picnic in the playroom around the puzzle board and we even found a few pieces each. We cleaned up and the kids had their baths and got in their PJ's and then went to watch TV and they had a brownie and milk for a snack.

***

26

The first day of school arrived and Lily Bear was so excited to go on the bus and Jamie was crying and clinging to me like a snuggle sheet. "Who am I gonna play with mommy?" My heart melted and I said, "I will play with you honey and don't forget that you have to take care of Sushi and Mochi too and they need you to play with them." Lily got right on the bus, no fuss, no muss and sat down in a window seat and waved goodbye like she has done it a million times before.

I didn't want to cry in front of Jamie and Vinnie knew I was close, so he took Jamie from me and handed me a tissue. Jamie saw me with tears in my eyes and he said, "You are sad Mommy?" I told him that I was going to miss Lily, but she would be back in a few hours. "I am ok Jamie." We all walked back up the driveway after the bus left and Vinnie went to work and Jamie and I played together in the playroom and we played with the kittens and then we went outside to play for a while. He was really feeling the loneliness without his sister. I kept him busy and before you know it, it was time for her bus to come so we walked to the end of the driveway and waited.

Jamie was so excited for her to come home. I picked him and held him, so there would be no running out in the road. The bus pulled up and Lily Bear came walking down the middle aisle and said goodbye to the bus driver and said, "See you next year." She got off the bus and I smiled at the bus driver. "Mommy, it was so much fun and I helped Mrs. Norton and I showed her my ABC's and she said it was very good." I responded. "Oh baby, that is so good. I am happy you had a good time and that you helped your teacher." The bus left and I put Jamie down and he hugged his sister. We walked up the driveway and she handed me some papers and I carried them into the house. I told her to go in her bedroom and put on her play clothes and then we would have lunch. She came out of her room and came into the kitchen with Jamie in tow. She said, "Mommy, when I go to school next year, will I be in number 1 grade?" I said, "Yes, but

first you have to finish Kindergarten this year."
She looked at me puzzled and said, "Mom, I
just did. I went to Kindergarten this year. I am
all done." I looked at her and knew this was
going to be a problem. She thought that she
only had to go one day. That's why she said
see you next year to the bus driver. Uh oh!!
Let's see if I can explain this to her.

"Honey, You have to go to Kindergarten every
day, except the weekends. Monday, Tuesday,
Wednesday, Thursday and Friday." She
looked at me and said, "No, I don't want to. I
finished Kindergarten." I said, "How come you
don't want to go? Tell me why?" She was so
serious and said, "Because I can't play with
Jamie and he is lonely." I told her that she has
to go to school and that I would play with
Jamie until she got home. She said, "No,
that's ok, I will stay home and play with him. I
am done with Kindergarten." I said, "Lily
Bear? Listen to mommy. You have to go to
school every day, except Saturday and Sunday
and you have to go to school from September
through June and then you have the summer

off and when you go back in September, you will be in First Grade." She looked at me and said, "No, I'm good. I don't want to go anymore." I just said, "Ok." I am going to leave this one for Vinnie, because he can get through to her more than I can. She has a thick head and she is the boss. This was his problem now, because I tried and got no where. I texted him to give him a heads up before he got home and he texted back. "Oh. My. God. This is gonna be bad."

Vinnie got home and she was waiting for him, along with Jamie. He swooped them both up in both arms and kissed them. He put them down and said, "So, Lily Bear, tell me about your first day of Kindergarten." She told him about helping her teacher and about writing the ABC's for her and said she had fun. He said, "So, are you going to help her tomorrow too and show her how you write your numbers?" Lily Bear looked puzzled at him and said, "Um No, I am gonna stay home and play with Jamie." He said, "Oh, is that right? I was just wondering who is going to help her tomorrow. I don't think there is anyone else there that can help, because you are the smartest little girl in the class." She just looked at him for a minute and then said, "Someone else can help her because I am staying home with Jamie." He said, "Ok, but I think she will be very, very sad that you aren't there with her. They might be doing story telling tomorrow and you will miss out on that. I think they would really love to hear the story about you saving the kittens in the bushes." She pondered on that for a little bit and said, "Mom, do you promise to play with Jamie tomorrow?" I looked at her and said, "I promise to play with him every day while you are at school." She looked at her father and said, "Well, Ok, I will go, if mom plays with Jamie, and I will tell my story about saving the kittens, but then I am coming home."

He told her that she would be going to school everyday and coming home everyday on the bus. She turned around without saying anything else and took Jamie into the playroom. I covered my mouth and turned my head so she wouldn't see me laughing.

Vinnie put his arm on my shoulder and turned me around. He kissed me and hugged me and said, "I missed you today. I want to do another weekend getaway and actually plan it this time." I was still in giggle mode from Lily, but I quickly ended that when I heard about a weekend getaway. "Oh, I am in on that action. Where to?" He said, "I was thinking the Poconos Mountains in Pennsylvania. Do you think your parents would spend a whole weekend here, until Monday?" I said, "I am sure they would love to." He said, "Oh good, because we are going. I set it up and we are leaving Friday afternoon." I was shocked. "Really? You are already did it?" He smiled and told me it was all planned. I called my parents and asked them if they could come Friday afternoon and stay until Monday night and they were so excited. "YES, YES, we would love to." I thanked them and told them we were going to the Poconos Mountains. Vinnie had to cancel our standing reservation for Saturday night.

Friday night was here before we knew it and we were all packed to go on our little Romantic getaway. He got a package deal, but we had to stay 3 nights, which was fine with me. We stayed at the Roman Tower. It had a 7 foot tall Champagne Glass Whirlpool, a private in-suite pool, a heart shaped whirlpool, an electric sauna and a round king-sized bed.

It had a fireplace and a sitting area and there were rose pedals and candles everywhere. We enjoyed the resort immensely, but we also visited the Poconos Indian Museum and the Snake and Animal Farm. We went to Klues Escape Room, but we couldn't get out. We did a trolley tour and visited the State Park. We went tubing, which was so much fun and neither of us had done this before. We went to an indoor waterpark and had a blast. We wished we had more time, but we didn't and Vinnie promised we would come back here, because there was so much to do and see.

The resort was gorgeous and our room got a lot of action, especially the champagne glass…and the heart shaped whirlpool…

We started home on Monday afternoon. It was a 3 hour ride and we wanted to be home before dark and before everyone got out of work, so we left at noon and we got home around 3:15. It was a pretty ride home and the leaves were starting to turn. We stopped at a roadside market and got some vegetables and corn and we saw cows, horses and goats and even a bunch of turkeys out in a field. We had such a good time together.

We kept in touch with my parents the whole time to make sure everything was going ok. Monday morning my mom called and said, "Lily didn't want to go to school today and no matter what I did, she gave me a hard time, so she is home."   I told her not to worry and we would take care of it when we got home.

Vinnie and I talked about the problem with school and he said, "I think it's time to be a little stern with her, because she has us wrapped around her little pinkie and it has to stop." He paused and then said, "She thinks she is the boss. Is that our fault?" I looked at him and said, "I think we are partly at fault, but I still think she will listen if we get a little stern and tell her how it's gonna be. We just have to let her know that we are the bosses and once she knows that, she will be ok."

We walked in the door and greeted everyone and picked the kids up to hug and kiss. My mom and dad were all packed up and we thanked them for babysitting and we gave them each a special gift from the Poconos gift shop.

Vinnie sat in the living room after we unpacked and Lily and Jamie climbed up in his lap and they were having a conversation about what they did with Gramma and Papa Madden this weekend and Lily did a lot of the talking. Then Vinnie said, "And what did you learn in school today Lily?" She looked at him and didn't answer. He said, "What did you learn today?" She said, "I didn't go to school today Daddy, because mommy wasn't here to play with Jamie." OMG this child was gonna kill me.

Vinnie looked at her and said, "Lily, from now on, you WILL go to school everyday, whether mommy is here or not. You are going and I don't want to hear anything more about it. Do you hear me?" She looked at him and said, "How come I have to?" He looked at her with a frown and said, "Because I SAID so. You are going to school every day because I said so.

Do you understand me?" She put her head down and said, "Yes". She got down off his lap and went to her room and closed the door. So now, we both felt guilty. We were going to let her stay for about a half hour and then we would go in, but she came out and didn't say a word. She crawled back up into her Daddy's lap and put her head on his shoulder. She lifted her head up and said, "Is tomorrow a school day Dad?" He shook his head yes and said, "Yes and you are going." She put her head back on his shoulder and whispered, "ok".

I knew this was not the end of this school shit. She listened to him, but would she listen to me tomorrow? Vinnie said he would stay until she got on the bus. She went to school because he was there, but on Wednesday, she gave me a hard time and Vinnie was at work. So I had to threaten her with a phone call to her father and then she got on the bus. I guess I had to get stern with her like Vinnie did. I hated doing it, but I <u>had </u>to do it. Once it was done, hopefully, we wouldn't have any more problems.

That afternoon, she got off the bus and told me she was going to walk to her friends house and she started walking. I grabbed her by her arm and said, "Lily, you are NOT going to walk anywhere and you are NOT allowed to do that, ever. Do you hear me?" She looked up at me and said, "But I want to." I tugged at her arm a little and said, "Get in the house Lily and don't push my buttons. You are not walking anywhere. I am the boss and you will do as you are told." She walked with me and didn't say anything else. When we got in the house, I said, "Go to your room and sit in your chair and don't come out until I say." She looked at me and I could tell she was pissed off, but so was I and I was not going to let her get away with this. After a half hour went by, I went in and she was sitting in her chair with her arms crossed. I sat on her bed and said, "Lily, do you know what you did wrong?" She didn't answer me. "I asked you a question, Lily Lorraine". She turned around to look at me and said, "Yes". I said, "I don't want you to ever talk to me like that again. Do you understand me?" She said, "Yes, but I am telling Daddy." I laughed at her and that pissed her off. "Well, Miss Lily Lorraine, you

go ahead and tell your Daddy, because you
know what he is gonna do when you tell him?"
She looked at me shocked and said, "What?"
I said, "He will probably punish you like I just
did, because he doesn't want you to talk to me
like that either. And he sure doesn't want you
walking to your friends house by yourself. You
are 5 years old and you are not allowed to do
that. Why are you misbehaving and being
mean to me? Did I do something to you to
make you mad?" She ran to me and said, "No
mommy, I love you and I am sorry mommy." I
asked her if someone in school or on the bus
was bothering her and she said no. She said,
"I just don't want to go to school anymore. I
want to stay home and play." I explained to
her that she is going to school to learn, so she
could be a doctor, like daddy, if she wanted to.
"If you stay home, then you won't learn
anything. You need to go to school to learn
and be smart." It was like a light bulb went off
and she said, "Ok, so if I go to school, I can be
a nurse or a doctor?" I told her she could be
anything she wanted to be, but she had to go
to school to learn. AND THAT, was the end of
the school shit.

I told Vinnie the whole story as we were laying in bed that night and he thought part of that story was funny, but the part where she said, she was going to walk to her friends house scared him. I told him it scared me too and I would always be out there when she got off the bus. He said he was going to have a talk with her in the morning. He said, "What is to stop her from getting off the bus at another stop?" I said, "Isn't the bus driver responsible for that?" He said he didn't know, but he was going to talk to the bus driver in the morning to make sure it didn't happen.

The next morning, Lily was ready for school and told her father she was going to learn how to be a doctor or a nurse. He smiled at her and said, "Come here. I want to talk to you before you go to school." She went over to him and he told her that she is never EVER allowed to walk to a friends house, because she was only 5 years old and that he would let her know when it was allowed. "Do you know that someone could grab you and take you home with them and you will never see mommy and daddy ever again? There are bad people out there Lily and it's dangerous to walk by yourself at 5 years old. I want you to promise me and mommy that you will never do that ok?" She said, "I promise."

Before she got on the bus, Vinnie got on the bus and sat behind the bus driver and had a short talk with her and explained what happened. She assured him that she never lets the kids get off at unauthorized stops. He felt better about that and thanked her. NOW THE SCHOOL SHIT WAS REALLY OVER!!

Lily straightened out after this incident and went to school every day, to learn. :) She knew we meant business and she wasn't going to get away with anything and Jamie watched and learned, so he knew too.

27

We were invited to Jimmy and Maria's house for Thanksgiving and they had my parents and Mary and Trevor and their parents. Everyone brought 2 or 3 dishes and we had oodles of food. Lily and Jamie made turkey sugar cookies that I let them make and they each had a dish to carry. I brought a yam casserole and a dutch apple pie with whipped cream. We really had a nice time together and the kids were playing with the Bengal kittens most of the day. Their names were Loki and Blaze. They were growing up fast and Bengals are bigger cats than the normal house cat.

We told the family about the school situation and the problems we had with Lily. Jimmie said, "I saw it coming. Just the way she was talking and telling stories. She thought she was the boss." He was laughing and said, "Good thing you nipped that in the bud." That was his favorite saying and now he had me saying it. He said, "She has a very strong personality and I see a big difference in her now, for the better." Vinnie told his brother that she was a nightmare for a while and he had no idea what to do or say to her. Jimmie laughed and said, "Thanks for letting me know what I am in for. Mine is right behind yours."

***

Lily graduated Kindergarten and she was so proud of herself, walking up to get her little diploma and so were we, sobbing in the audience and taking pictures and video. She came to sit with us after the ceremony and told her father that she was going to be a doctor because she finished school. I just rolled my eyes because I felt another shit storm coming. Vinnie just said, "Congratulations on finishing Kindergarten Lily Bear. Next year, you will be in First Grade."

She said, "But I will be a doctor before I go to First Grade?" Vinnie said, "Honey, it takes a long time to become a doctor. You have to go keep going to school and continue to learn things and then when you are done with that, you have to go to college. Mommy and I went to college to become doctor's assistants."

She looked at me and said, "Mommy, you are a doctor?" I smiled at her and said, "I am a doctor's assistant, like Daddy." She was totally confused now. "How come you don't go to work like Daddy?" I tried to explain that I am staying home with my babies to take care of them and when they get older, I will go back to work.

Vinnie told her that we studied and went to college together every single night and then had to take a big test to get our license. She looked at Vinnie and said, "I am gonna do that too." And then she turned to Jamie and said, "Will you be a doctor with me and study with me Jamie?" He said, "I don't wanna be a doctor." She tilted her head at him and said, "How come? What do you want to be?" He shrugged his shoulders and said, "I don't know yet, but it won't be a doctor." Vinnie and I were looking at each other and smiling, almost laughing.

28

I told Vinnie later that night that the school thing was not over and he agreed that come September, there would be more problems. He said we should take a family vacation this summer and he was thinking Disney for the kids. I got all excited and said, "Kids? I have never been there either. I am in." He looked at me and said, "NEVER? You have never been to Disney babe?" I shook my head no. "No, we never went there. We only took weekend trips to Connecticut, New Hampshire, Pennsylvania and surrounding states. When we went to Florida, that was my first time there." He looked shocked and said, "I never knew that. You never said anything about it." I told him I was excited to Disney, but I wanted to keep it a secret from the kids till we got there, or maybe buy them Disney luggage or do something else cool to tell them. He liked that idea and said we would figure out something. He told me that he went to Disney twice when he was a kid and once as a teenager. "You will love it there. It's a fairy tale."

Vinnie set up the trip and we were going to spend two weeks there so the kids could see everything. He said we could visit Sea World too, if I wanted to do three weeks. I told him I was never there either. "Let's do it. We will be down there, so we might as well." I was so excited to go on vacation for three weeks. Vinnie had the time, so he was going to use it and he had time to use around Christmas too. He gave his vacation notice to the Crowleys and they were happy that he was taking vacation.   Vinnie rented a two-bedroom Villa that was close to Sea World and Disney. We had a Hot Tub and heated pool. We had our own kitchen and living room and the kids would share a room and they had their own beds. The package that he got had free park shuttles and free fast passes, with complimentary breakfast buffet. This was going to be so much fun.

We were leaving in 2 weeks at the beginning of July. We asked my Mom and Dad and his Mom and Dad to take turns taking care of Sushi and Mochi. They would each stay for a week and a half to care for the cats.

My Mom and Dad came over to babysit the kids while Vinnie and I went shopping at the mall to get vacation clothes and luggage for the kids. We went into the Disney store and a few other stores and we got them a few bathing suits, shorts and T-shirts. We got Jamie a couple pairs of dress pants and nice tops to go out for dinner and we got Lily a few nice dresses and sandals.

We bought them new pajamas and Mickey Mouse water bottles, small toothpastes and new toothbrushes. We found Mickey and Minnie suitcases on wheels and they came with little backpacks and little wallets inside, so we got them. We bought them Mickey and Minnie beach towels and we even found Mickey and Minnie flip flops. Vinnie asked for a couple of huge bags for the suitcases and we put everything in the suitcases that we bought for them and put the suitcases in the big bags.

I think I was more excited for this trip than they would be. We took everything home and brought it up in the bedroom. Later on, we would take everything out, take the tags off and arrange everything in the suitcases and put them back in. We also bought stuff for ourselves because I needed a new bathing suit and flip flops and so did Vinnie. He got a new pair of black dress pants and a new shirt and I got a dress and sandals. We bought all the travel size things that we needed and also a couple of water bottles. We already had our luggage so we were all set.

I asked Vinnie when we were going to surprise them and he said, "No time like the present. I will take video and you take pictures." I carried a bag and he carried a bag and we went downstairs. I told my Mom and Dad to stay for dinner because we were getting take out and we wanted them to see the kids opening their luggage. The kids saw the bag and they were wondering what was going on. Vinnie gave Jamie his bag and I gave Lily Bear her bag and told them to wait because we wanted to take pictures and video. Ready, SET, GO! They took the luggage out of the bag and had puzzled looks on their faces. I said, "Open it." They opened it and started taking stuff out and Vinnie said, "Do you know where you are going yet?" Lily got a look on her face and said, "Vacation Daddy?" Vinnie laughed and said, "Yes, where do you think we are going?" Jamie screamed, "TO SEE MICKEY MOUSE?"

And then it dawned on Lily and she screamed, "DISNEY WORLD TO SEE MINNIE?" Vinnie was practically crying. "Yup, we are all taking a vacation to Disney and we leave next week."

They both started jumping up and down and hugging us and screaming. My Mom was crying and my Dad was a little emotional. Lily got a sad look on her face and stopped jumping up and down and she said, "Dad, I can't go because I have my kitties to take care of." Vinnie smiled at her and said, Your Grammies and Papa's are going to take care of your kitties." The smile returned and she was all excited.

For the next week, we all prepared for our vacation. I was packing last minute things for the kids like socks and underwear, brushes and sneakers. Vinnie and I had our suitcases open on the bench in our bedroom and we were putting things in as we thought of them and we had an empty fold up case for souvenirs.

We were leaving on Friday morning and Vinnie got us a limo to the airport. This would be the first time the kids went on a plane, not to mention this was their first vacation. I brought dramamine, just in case. Vinnie got 2 seats on one side of the plane and 2 seats right across the aisle on the other side. He would sit with Jaime and I would sit with Lily.

Of course, they could switch if they wanted to. We were hoping it wouldn't be a packed flight. The kids were downstairs and dragging their suitcases around and thought they were the cat's meow. Lily was showing Jamie how to do it and he just looked at her and said, "You don't have to show me, I am not stupid." He was definitely growing up and he was tired of being pushed around by Lily and it was showing. They still got along famously all the time, but he wasn't going to let her tell him what to do or how to do it, anymore.

Vinnie had so many things planned for us when we got there and he was definitely excited to take us all on vacation to a place we have never been before. Our limo arrived and his parents were all settled in for a week and a half and then my parents would take over till we got home. The kids got in and they were overwhelmed at the size of it and how big the inside was. They had orange juice boxes in there for the kids and we sipped on mimosa's. What a great beginning of a vacation! We got to the airport and the kids were told not to let go of our hands for even a second. We went to the food court to get some breakfast and then we found our Gate B-7 and sat down with them. Vinnie took Jamie to the bathroom and I took Lily, just before we boarded and we hoped that we wouldn't have to take them during the flight. We got on the plane and they were both wide-eyed and couldn't believe the inside of the plane. They got to meet the pilot and got their wings during the flight. They were both very good and no one needed dramamine.

We let the kids sit near the windows so they could see out and we got some good pics of them seeing the wonders of the world.

This was all new to them and they were amazed by all of it. They had some juice and cookies during the flight and they watched cartoons on the inflight TV. There was no one sitting next to Vinnie and no one sitting next to me, so the kids went back and forth, but we made them wear their seatbelts.

Then it was time to land and I think the landing scared Jamie a little because he was stuck to Vinnie like glue. Lily didn't let on, but I think she was too, so I held her hand.

We had a limo waiting for us at the airport that took us to our Villa. We got the kids settled into their bedroom with their suitcases and backpacks and they were fascinated by the twin beds with Minnie and Mickey bedspreads and pillows. They had Mickey and Minnie bars of soap and washcloths in their bathroom. Vinnie and I took pictures of all of it before they messed it all up. Lily kept saying, "This is awesome, just so awesome." We got settled in ourselves and we ordered room service to get lunch and the kids wanted to go in the pool, but Vinnie told them, that would be later. "We are going to see Cirque du Soleil, Drawn to Life, and it starts in about an hour and a half, so we have to clean up here and then get ready for our ride there." They were asking all kinds of questions about what it was and why we were going there when we were supposed to be going to Disney…. Vinnie explained that this was a special show in Disney and they will love it.

We got our ride and went to see the show. If I could only explain their faces as they watched the show, I would, but I got more enjoyment out of watching them watch the show than the actual show. They were stunned and amazed and it showed. They were the quietest, I ever saw them. They watched in amazement and I saw Vinnie looking at them too and he was smiling. This was a great pick for them. They saw all their favorite characters come alive and they couldn't believe it. We got some great pictures of them watching the show too. They clapped at the end and it was adorable. Vinnie got them on video.

He asked them in the limo going back to the villa, if they enjoyed the show and they both were talking at the same time and they were still excited about it. Vinnie told them to take turns taking a shower and we set their clothes out for them and he said we were going out to dinner.

We got back in the limo and we went to Planet Hollywood at Disney Springs. The kids got light-up drinks and they thought that was the best thing ever and Chicken Fingers with French Fries and piece of Chocolate layer Cake for dessert.

While they were eating, they were watching the big screen TV with Children's movies and they had sing alongs and they were singing to the songs. They had a blast. Vinnie and I got a Nacho appetizer and the kids nibbled on that too. I got the Bacon Mac and Cheese Burger with Fries and Cheese, which was friggin awesome. Vinnie got Penne Chicken & Broccoli, which I tasted and it was outstanding. We both got the Brownie Sundae Martini. We stayed to watch the rest of a children's movie and then went back to the villa.

We all got into our bathing suits and went in to the huge pool to go swimming and just relax. The kids were having a blast. This was only day one and we had 3 weeks. Vinnie and I decided that we wanted to take a couple of days out of that time and spend it at the Villa.

It had the pool and a bbq and a hammock and things for the kids to do. We had the kitchen and the living room too. Vinnie told them that tomorrow we were going to Disney's Animal Kingdom.

They were out like lights when they hit the pillow that night. We were all up at 8:00 and went for our free breakfast and the kids filled up with Mickey pancakes and bacon and orange juice and Vinnie and I had scrambled eggs, sausage and coffee.

Next stop was the Animal Kingdom and they met Moana at Character Landing and saw the Tree of Life. There were over 300 animal carvings in it and you could stand there looking at them for ages. They saw Finding Nemo: The Big Blue…and Beyond. It was actually a puppet show. We went on a Na'vi River Journey. It was a mystical journey by boat through Pandora's glowing bioluminescent rainforest. It was the most beautiful boat ride ever. It was extraordinary and we went through a series of caves and saw exotic plants and creatures on all sides, even overhead. The music was legendary and was supposed to send positive energy out into the forest through the power of the music.

We went to the Tusker House Restaurant for lunch and the kids saw Donald Duck, Mickey and Pluto, along with some other Disney friends. The kids had a cake that looked like a

Mickey hat and they were thrilled with it. We went to see Donald Duck's Dino Bash which was a prehistoric party. Donald just found out that some of his ancestors were dinosaurs. Chip and Dale were in attendance too. We went to the Adventure Outpost and the kids got to see Mickey and Minnie.

The kids had a full day here and now we were heading back to the Villa for showers and then out to dinner.   We were taking them to the Rainforest Cafe. We took the limo to the Cafe and I have to say that I never imagined it to be as wonderful as they said. I was as amazed as my kids. I think Vinnie got a picture of me with my eyes wide. We all walked around to see everything before we got seated. I kept looking around at everything and couldn't decide what to eat. For an appetizer, we got a sampler and the kids ate it with us. I finally decided on Jungle Steak and Shrimp and Vinnie got Mojo Bones, which was a half rack of pork spareribs with smokin' mojo BBQ sauce, coleslaw and Safari fries. The kids got the BBQ Bacon Cheeseburger. We were all too full for dessert, so Vinnie order a Sparking Volcano to go, which was a giant chocolate brownie stacked high, served warm with vanilla ice cream and whipped topping, caramel and chocolate sauces. It didn't last long because we ate it all when we got to the Villa. Of course the ice cream was melted, but it was friggin delicious. Day 2 was done and the kids were tired, but they wanted to go in the pool, so Vinnie told them 15 minutes. They both went in to change and they never came out. They were passed out on their beds in their bathing suits. LOL. We just put them under the comforter and left them. AHHH.

We had a little alone time. We ordered a bottle of wine from room service and indulged a bit and enjoyed each other and then just watched TV. We were tired too and we dozed off pretty early.

Day 3 was Fantasia Gardens Miniature Golf Course. We went for breakfast and then got going. This place was amazing too. Of course, every place we went to, was amazing.

This was an 18-hole miniature golf adventure based on Disney's animated film Fantasia. There were fountains and musical surprises.

They had a sign saying Beware of the broomsticks. They will douse golfers who pass below. There were hippos wearing Tu-Tu's, pirouetting ostriches and marching broomsticks. We were here for a couple of hours and the kids were playing a good game of golf for their first time. They were fascinated with the whole place and so was I. We were doing Magic Kingdom for a few days because there was so much to see, so we waited until we got these other places out of the way. Vinnie wanted them to see Typhoon Lagoon. It was a water park and he knew they would have a blast here. That was going to be tomorrow.

We went out for dinner at the Nine Dragons Restaurant to have some Chinese Chow. We started with an assortment of Spring Rolls and Pot Stickers. We got the kids the Moo Goo Gai Pan and they split that. That is stir fried chicken, snow peas, carrots and mushrooms.

They ate this at home, so we figured they would eat it here and they really loved it. It was made a little different, but they still loved it.   Vinnie and I ordered Fried rice and he got Kung Pao Shrimp and I got the Kung Pao Chicken. We didn't eat dessert there because the kids didn't like anything they saw, so we took them out for ice cream at a place called, Beaches & Cream Soda Shop. They both got a waffle cone with their favorite ice cream. When we got in there, we realized that they had lunch and dinner food, so we decided we would come back here again to eat before we left. The place was decorated in bright colors and had long thin lights hanging from the ceiling and they were changing colors. The tables were round with a big white pedestal underneath and the chairs were a lime green with different colors seats, some green, some peach and some yellow. It really was a pretty place and it was very clean and the staff was friendly. Vinnie and I were very impressed with this little place.

We got back to the Villa and the kids went swimming for about a half hour and got out without us telling them to because they were exhausted. They didn't even ask where we were going tomorrow. They hit the pillows and they were out!

Day 4 was the Typhoon Lagoon Water Park. We all got up and went to eat our free breakfast and got our free ride to the waterpark. The kids had no idea what to expect and to be honest, we didn't either. This place was inside the Magic Kingdom Park and as we were entering, you go through an arch that has Mickey on one side and Minnie on the other, with stars and lights and rainbows and all kinds of lights flashing in all different colors. You should have seen the looks on their faces as we went underneath the arch.

We used our fast passes and first went on the Crush n' Gusher. It was a coaster like raft ride for 2, so each of us took one of the kids and went down. Me and Lily were screaming the whole way down and Vinnie went with Jamie and I think they were screaming too!! We took them to Ketchakiddee Creek. This was for little ones and it had a water playground with pint-sized slides and water cannons. They really loved this one. We rented Huge tubes and went tubing.

We stopped for lunch at a place called Leaning Palms and got hotdogs and pizza. The kids had soda and Vinnie and I got a beer. Then it was off to Happy Landings Ice Cream, where the kids got Mickey's Ice Cream Sandwich. Vinnie and I got a Frozen Lemonade Cup. Yum!! We stayed at the Lagoon for the whole day because the kids were having so much fun. We were coming back to the Magic Kingdom for the rest of the week to ride the rides and see the sites. There was so much to see at this park and we wanted to make sure they saw all the important things.

Day 5 was mostly rides. We went to Fantasy Land and the kids went on the Alice in Wonderland ride, Peter Pan's Flight, the Mad Tea Party, Mr. Toad's Wild Ride and It's a Small World (after all). We went to Big Thunder Mountain Railroad and went on a Mine Train Roller Coaster. The kids wanted to go on Space Mountain, but Vinnie and I thought it was a bit too much for them. It was more for grown-ups. I didn't even want to go on it. LOL. They went on the Dumbo the Flying Elephant ride. That was gentle flying carousel ride. They loved the Magic Carpets of Aladdin.

They got to ride a magic carpet and the people in the front row, which was us, controlled how high the carpet goes. They really loved Buzz Lightyear Space Range. It was a slow ride and they got to fire lasers and earn points to defeat the Evil Emperor Zurg, as they journeyed through a Galactic Space battle. It really was a cute ride. They went on it 3 times.

We left there to go out to get something to eat and decided to go back to the Beaches and Cream Soda Shop and had a nice little dinner there and of course ice cream to finish it off. The kids thought the day was over, but Vinnie had other plans for all of us.

We headed back to Magic Kingdom in the dark and we saw the Main Street Electrical Parade. There were thousands of lighted floats and live performances on the floats. Vinnie told me that there were over 600,000 electronically controlled LED lights that were synchronized with a sound track that was triggered by radio control. They saw Mickey, Minnie, Pluto, The Jungle Book Characters, Pinocchio, Cinderella, Alice in Wonderland, Snow White and the Seven Dwarfs, Dumbo, Goofy and the Toy Story characters, along with thousands of other characters. At the very end of the parade, there were tons and tons of fireworks. They lasted for over a half hour and they were beautiful. Vinnie took video of some of it and I got some good photos. Lily looked at me and Vinnie when it was over and said, "This was the bestest day ever." She had tears in her eyes. And you know, that brought tears to my eyes. It meant a lot to Vinnie too and he got a little emotional. He really outdid himself with this trip and this was only week one. We still had 2 weeks to go. I am sure he spent tons of money, because this trip was NOT cheap. Although he said he got really good deals and free passes and all that stuff, still, the dinners alone were expensive. He told me that he has been saving for it for a long time and shushed me.

Day 6 was another day at Magic Kingdom. Lily had lunch at Cinderella's Royal Table and sat with Princess Jasmine, Snow White, Princess Ariel and Princess Aurora. I stayed with her, while Vinnie took Jamie to lunch at a place next door. We could actually see each other.

We went on a couple different rides with our fast passes in-between lunch and dinner. The Roller Coaster rides at Disney were slow and kid friendly. There were only a few that were for adults or teens.

Dinner was very exciting for both of them. They got to have dinner with Mickey and Minnie and they had their pictures taken with them. They got stuffed Mickey's and Minnie's and the characters signed them for the kids. Lily said, "This was the next bestest day ever Daddy."

Day 7 was going to be the next bestest day for them both because we were taking them to Goofy's Kitchen for lunch. This was in a Disneyland Hotel and it was an all you can eat buffet. All the characters were there and they were waiting on the tables. Getting drinks for the kids and adults and taking pictures with the kids. It was so much fun for them. There were no 'people' working there. It was just the characters, which I thought was the greatest idea ever for the kids. They both loved it and kept saying it was the bestest day ever.

After lunch, we went to visit Cinderella's Castle. It is 189 feet tall and the most beautiful castle you will ever see. We walked through it and on the inside, was the Disney family Coat of Arms, and it was displayed with intricate mosaic murals, made of over a million pieces of Italian glass in over 500 colors. On the second floor (I never knew this) is Cinderella's Royal Table Restaurant. You need Advance Dining Reservations for this place and we did not have it. I guess the reservations have to be made months in advance. Cinderella and several of her princess friends attend the meals and pose for photos with the guests.

Next on Vinnie's list was the Lightning McQueen's Racing Academy show. It puts you in the middle of the Disney and Pixar Cars universe. Lightning demonstrates what he's learned over the years by using his brand-new, state of the art racing stimulator and its wraparound screen, but he finds out that things don't always go according to plan and he has to think fast to get back on course. He has Tow Mater, Cruz Ramirez and the gang from Radiator Springs rooting him on. The kids were so into this show. I can't tell you if he wins because that will just spoil it for you if you go to see it.

Next was Mickey & Minnie's Runaway Railway. At the beginning of the ride, we were invited to watch the premiere of a new Mickey Mouse cartoon, Perfect Picnic, in which Mickey and Minnie Mouse prepare for a picnic outing and encounter Goofy driving a train. Then we passed through a simulated movie screen where we experienced a zippy zany out-of-control adventure. Then we were transported into the cartoon and aboard Goofy's train, which took us on a wild adventure. This was really the most original ride I ever saw and I enjoyed it as much as the kids. I think they were a little scared at first, but then realized it was all fake.

For dinner we went to the Cape May Cafe and we got the Seafood-and-more-Dinner Buffet which included Shrimp, Clams, Lemon Chicken, slow roasted Strip Loin and crab legs. The kids got a special souvenir character cup with Minute Maid Zero Sugar Lemonade with flavors of Cotton Candy and they had Roasted Chicken with mashed potatoes and a vegetable. Vinnie and I stuffed ourselves with the buffet.

We headed to the Villa after that and we all went for a dip in the pool and then in to watch TV and relax. The kids were sleeping by 8:00 p.m. Vinnie thought they could do with a day of rest, so we spent Day 8 at the Villa. We ate the free breakfast and we went and got stuff for lunch and dinner. We let them go in the pool and they had a playground that we let them play on, but they really weren't interested in doing anything else because they were exhausted. It was a good day to relax and it actually rained all afternoon. It stopped just in time to barbecue some dinner. Nothing fancy, just a couple of steaks and some veggie skewers. I think we all needed some downtime. The weather said it was supposed to rain tomorrow too, so we might have another day of downtime. We still had plenty of time to see everything we wanted to. Day 9 rained all day and we ordered food in because it was raining cats and dogs and there was no way we could bbq and who wants to cook on vacation anyway?

It was good downtime. They had games in the room and we played them and some card games. They had an indoor playroom and we took the kids down for a while to see what it was like. After the week they just had, the playroom was boring. LOL. They stayed for a bit and went down the slide a few times. They had rubber sand in the room so the kids wouldn't get hurt. I have never seen anything like that. We walked around and found an indoor heated pool and we decided to use it, so we all went back to the villa and got changed. We spent a couple hours there and everyone had fun. We didn't know the pool was there and no one was in it. I checked with someone first to make sure we could use it and they said it was included. So we had the whole pool to ourselves. We went back to the Villa and showered and got comfortable and we ordered dinner in.

It was Day 10 and the weather was beautiful, so we were back to the Magic Kingdom. Daddy had a surprise for the kids today. He had made reservations for them at Bibbidi Bobbidi Boutique where they would be transformed into a Princess and a Knight. Lily picked the Royal Braid with flowers, a pink shimmery gown and she had her makeup done, pink nail polish and fancy gold lace-up sandals, and she really looked like Daddy's little Princess. Jamie picked a knight costume and got a fancy hairstyle with glitter, a sword and a shield. He was Mommy's knight in shining armor. The transformation takes about an hour and a half, but it was well worth it. They take professional pictures and we had them taken separately and then together.

By the time this was all done and the pictures were taken, it was almost time for lunch, so we just walked around for a bit to see what we were going to do after lunch. We decided that after lunch we would go to the Haunted Mansion and see what that was all about.

We walked into a place called Sleepy Hollow and we all got hand-dipped corn dogs with house made chips and some water. The kids wanted soda, but they have been having soda all week, so water it was.

We headed over to the Haunted Mansion and Vinnie told the kids that it was all fake and it may seem scary sometimes, but not to worry about it and they seemed fine. It was a slow-ride and it was in the dark and there was a ghost voice talking the whole time. We were gliding by a casket filled conservatory,

Madame Leota's chilling seance room, a crypt, a leaky tomb, a few creepy things and a ghostly graveyard of singing dead people. I didn't think it was that scary and the kids didn't think so either, which was good. It was a little creepy, but not scary.

We then went to Mickey's Town Square Theater, where the kids saw Mickey again and had their picture taken with him. He did some magic for them and made a dove and rabbit disappear and the looks on their faces were priceless.

They were getting tired of walking and so were we, so we headed back to the Villa to rest for the day. Day 10 was a really busy day for them and they didn't even want to go swimming. They showered and got into their pj's before we even had dinner. We ordered a couple of pizza's and we let them eat it in the living room.

On Day 11, we decided that after breakfast, we would make one last trip to the Magic Kingdom and do a few things and go on a few rides, have lunch and then call it a day.

We went to the Disney Festival of Fantasy Parade. It started right after we got there and I think it was the last time until later on. It was only 12 minutes or so long and there were tons of floats and music and Disney Characters like Peter Pan, the characters from Tangled and The Little Mermaid. The kids loved this parade, the music was loud and they were singing the songs with them.

Next was the Jungle Cruise. It was a river cruise where dangerous beast were seen. It was a steamer that was piloted by our trusty skipper who navigated us through the world's most treacherous waters. There were hippo's, hungry lions and sleeping zebras along the Nile. There was lush foliage, butterflies and waterfalls on the Amazon in South America. We saw an abandoned camp that was overrun by Gorillas on the shores of the African Congo. It was a 10 minute, 10,000 mile journey that none of us will ever forget.

Next was the Avatar Flight of Passage, where you climbed atop a winged mountain banshee for a 3D flight over Pandora's landscape. Bonding with your Banshee is a crucial step in the life of a Na'vi hunter on Pandora. You get an up-close look at this moon's landscape.

You are flying on the back of one of these powerful creatures and you are a visitor of Pandora and you finally have the chance to test yourself like a Na'vi. The kids liked the 3D part of this, but they were a little too young to understand it. Vinnie and I enjoyed it though.

It was lunchtime and we walked around to find a different place for lunch. We went to this great place called the T-Rex Cafe and the restaurant looked like a cave and it had a T-Rex skeleton over the top of it. It was so cool looking and the kids were speechless when they saw it. This place was the best so far. There were brightly colored jelly fish and starfish hanging from the ceiling and a huge octopus that hung over the whole bar. It was all lit up with bright blue's and pinks.

There were all kinds of dinosaurs, all different colors and sizes. All the food was named after dinosaurs or the era of dinosaurs and if you bought a drink in a glass you got to take the glass home. So you know, we did. It had a T-Rex on it with their logo. We got the supersaurus sampler for an appetizer. The kids got Prehistoric Pasta with Chicken, I got the Pork-asaurus sandwich and Vinnie got the Paleozoic Chicken Sandwich. It was very expensive here, but Vinnie didn't care. He wanted everyone to have fun and enjoy the vacation. You were paying for the ambience more than the food and it was well worth it.

We headed back to the Villa for the rest of the day and Day 12 would start our Sea World Adventure. The kids went in the pool for a while and then settled in to relax and watch some cartoons on TV.

Days 12 through 18 we spent at Sea World. We thought we needed more time to see everything, but we didn't. We saw everything in 7 days. We took our time, because we had it. The kids loved this place and thoroughly enjoyed it. We all saw the Dolphin Encounter, the Dolphin Nursery, Flamingo Cove, the Alligator Habitat, the Empire of the Penguin, We dined with the Orca's, we went to the Jewel of the Sea Aquarium, the Mantee Rehab Area, Manta Aquarium, we saw the Orca's Underwater, the Pacific Point Preserve, the Pelican Preserve, SeaWorld Coral Rescue Center, the Shark Encounter, StingRay Lagoon and the Wild Arctic.

We went on rides on the last day of our trip there. They went on the Sesame Streetland, Elmo's Choo Choo Train, Rubber Duckie Water Works, the Sunny Day Carousel and we all did the Flamingo Paddle Boats. I think the paddle boats was everyones favorite.

Day 19 Vinnie and I took the kids to Discovery Cove. It was a tropical paradise that was incredible. We snorkeled with the Tropical Fish and Rays and we went to the Aviary where we all got to feed Exotic Birds. They actually ate out of our palms from little cups of food. We bought the day pass, so all our food for the day was free. We went on the Lazy River Ride and we ate at the Blue Bamboo and the Hibiscus Hideaway. It was a fantastic day.

On Day 20, we drove over to the coast and went to Clearwater Beach and spent the day there and on Day 21, our vacation was over. We packed up all our treasures and clothes and headed for the airport. The kids actually fell asleep on the plane and I think I dozed off too.

It felt good to be home and the kids missed their kitties and I think they were glad to be home too. My mom and dad were all packed and said the cats were no problem at all. The kids gave their grandparents all the gifts we bought them and they showed them all the stuff they got and they talked for hours. We invited them to stay for dinner at that point because the talking did not stop. LOL

Vinnie called his parents to let them know we were home safe and asked if they wanted to come over for dinner and said my parents were here and we were gonna order out.

They accepted and were at the house in 15 minutes. Vinnie ordered a bunch of stuff from the restaurant down the street and had it delivered. The kids did nothing but talk about their vacation. All the grandparents got their little souvenirs and got their ears talked off. We showed them some pictures and we had a nice time. I was really looking forward to my shower, PJ's and my own bed. I was so tired from all the traveling.

29

***

I was sitting in my chair in the living room and just happened to look out the window to see two red cardinals, sitting right outside the window on the sill and looking in. I said out loud, "Hi Rain, I see you found your boyfriend. I told you that you would." I waved at them and a few seconds later, they flew away. I never saw them again and I think she just wanted to let me know she was ok and that she found someone. Mary told me that a pair of cardinals visited her as well and then she never saw them again.

When the kids turned 16, I went back to work at Crowley & Crowley, M.D. with Vinnie, because they lost their physician assistant and they were happy to have me back.

Many, many years went by and my Lily Bear was in college and studying to be a doctor. She said she would be, a long time ago and she never changed her mind.

She had on-line classes, as well as going to the college itself. She was in the top of her class. Little Miss Sassy pants really grew up and was very respectful of us and I was so proud of her.

My little Jamie was little no more and was almost as tall as Vinnie and towered over me. He was such a gentleman, like his Dad. He was studying to be an electrical engineer and wanted nothing to do with the medical field. He was such a good boy. I was so proud of him.

Jimmie and Maria had another child after Ruthie Renee, by accident. It was another little girl and she was 5 years younger than Ruthie. They named her Mary.

Kyle was also taking college courses to become an accountant and Ruthie was taking courses to become a paralegal. Mary is now in high school.

Trevor died of a heart attack a few years ago and Mary was living alone, next door to my mom and dad. They offered to have her live with them, but she said she would be ok on her own.

We all went to Delaware for Trevor's funeral and he was being buried next to Rain. I visited her grave, while I was there and there was a red cardinal feather on top of her stone. I don't know what that meant, but I hoped that it was from her boyfriend or maybe that Trevor was now a cardinal?

My mom and dad are doing well, minus the old age aches and pains, but nothing major and they still visit us all the time.

Vinnie's parents are also doing well too. And like my parents, had the old age aches and pains, which I do not look forward to. We had them over all the time for dinner with my parents and Mary.

Sushi and Mochi were still doing well and Lily still took care of them. I told her that we could take over and she said, "I promised to be their mom a long time ago. That is not something that can be changed mom."

Vinnie and I went on vacation every summer to a different place and enjoyed each other so much. We went back to Disney one other time with the kids before they started college and they still had the same look on their faces.

I will always remember the day I met my Vinnie. He came to rescue me and when I asked him why he was still there, he told me that I caught his eye and he promised me that he would make me happy and protect me for the rest of my life and he kept his promise. I caught his eye and he caught my heart and that will never change… 🤍 💕 🤍

ACKNOWLEDGEMENT

Thank you Chrissy. You continue to amaze me by reading my stories, night after night and editing with me. For someone who doesn't like to read, you have read all 7 of my books and I feel honored.

www.ingramcontent.com/pod-product-compliance
Lightning Source LLC
Chambersburg PA
CBHW050721260726
48661CB00001B/13